FLYING IN THE FACE
OF TRADITION

· · · · · ·

Listening to the Lived Experience
of the Faithful

· · · · · ·

Louis DeThomasis, FSC

acta
PUBLICATIONS

FLYING IN THE FACE OF TRADITION
Listening to the Lived Experience of the Faithful
by Louis DeThomasis, FSC

Edited by Gregory F. Augustine Pierce
Cover design by Tom A. Wright
Text design and typesetting by Patricia A. Lynch
Copyright © 2012 by Louis DeTomasis

Published by ACTA Publications, 4848 N. Clark Street, Chicago, IL 60640, (800) 397-2282, www.actapublications.com

Library of Congress Catalog Number: 2011946192
Hardcover ISBN: 978-0-87946-484-4
Paperback ISBN: 978-0-87946-485-1
Printed in the United States of America by McNaughton & Gunn, Inc.
Year 20 19 18 17 16 15 14 13 12
Printing 12 11 10 9 8 7 6 5 4 3

CONTENTS

DEDICATION

To Saint John Baptist De LaSalle and his Brothers,
as Jesus lives in their hearts forever!
And to my brother "Luddy,"
as he is now in the loving embrace of the Lord forever!

A NOTE FROM THE PUBLISHER

The job of the publisher is simply to give good authors an outlet for their ideas. That is what we have done here with Brother Louis DeThomasis' provocative book, *Flying in the Face of Tradition*. I urge you to read it in the spirit with which it is written, one of passion, concern, and hope for the Catholic Church that he loves.

Brother Louis is not some alienated Catholic out to do the church harm. Just the opposite. He has been a moderate, well-respected De LaSalle Brother and Christian educator and investment manager for more than forty years. He was president and professor of Interdisciplinary Studies at Saint Mary's University of Minnesota from 1984 to 2005 and the co-founder and former president of the Christian Brothers Investment Services (CBIS), which helps many Catholic organizations benefit from a managed portfolio based on Catholic principles and values. He is currently the president of CBIS-GLOBAL: Europe. He has received many awards and recognition of his service to the church and society, including the *Pro Ecclesia et Pontifice Award* conferred by Pope John Paul II in 1998, knighthood in the Equestrian Order of the Holy Sepulchre of Jerusalem in 1989, and five honorary degrees from five U.S. colleges and universities.

So you see that Brother Louis is, in a way, a member of the "institutional church" that he calls to account and transformation. He does so not with any malice or mean-spiritedness but rather with a sense of clarity, urgency, and love. He knows, as do we, that several members of the institutional church have demanded that some of the issues he raises, specifically the ordination of women, are "closed" and never to be discussed again. However, using the church's own teaching of the role of the lived experience of the faithful as a continuing source of revelation and renewal in the church, he respectfully offers his own thoughts as "an exercise in tradition."

ACTA Publications, which has its own fifty-plus years of contributions to the church, has always been a publishing house where dialogue is encouraged and innovation is developed. We feel that Brother Louis is offering a fresh and insightful contribution to what is happening in the church and in the world right now and how we may "unravel the quandary" that the institutional church is facing, whether it admits it or not.

Don't take my word for it. Read and decide for yourself whether or not Brother Louis makes sense. The Holy Spirit will be with you as you do so, because Jesus promised to send forth the Spirit "to fill the hearts of the faithful."

Gregory F. Augustine Pierce
President and Co-Publisher
ACTA Publications

INTRODUCTION

Unraveling the Quandary before It Unravels Us

• • • • • •

This is our joy:
that through the living river of tradition
Christ is not 2,000 years away from us
but is truly with us always.

POPE BENEDICT XVI

• • • • • •

The word *tradition* is a critical element in the Roman Catholic Church's understanding of itself. This book is an attempt to go beyond an intuitive understanding of that word and seek to rediscover in it a blueprint for unraveling the quandary taking place in the church today, before the institutional church itself unravels.

I do not intend to make this a theological treatise on tradition. I am not a theologian. Rather, my aim is to appeal to common sense and the core values and beliefs within Catholicism to offer some carefully derived conclusions regarding two important factors: first, an understanding of the present reality of what is going on in the world today; and second, an analysis of how that present reality affects what is going on within the church today.

Throughout the book I refer to "the church" or "the Catholic Church" and use the two terms interchangeably. Specifically I am referring to the Roman Catholic Church, of which I am a lifelong member and a professed religious. Yet the audience I am attempting to reach with these conclusions is not only those situated on the inside of the institutional Roman Catholic Church or its academic community *per se*. I definitely hope this work will have something to say to them; but at least as importantly I hope to reach the wider audience of faithful Catholics who are deeply troubled at this moment in the history of the church. Finally, it seems important that I try to reach a wider spectrum of Christians in general.

As I wrote this book I kept in my mind a unique lesson in academic scholarship and integrity from my undergraduate days in the late 1950s. I was working on my bachelor's degree at Georgetown University's Edmund A. Walsh School of Foreign Service. On the first day of his class, one of the most scholarly and beloved Jesuit professors of the time provided us with a unique insight.

• • • • • •

I love the Catholic Church and have always been thoroughly committed to it to this day.

• • • • • •

He said that the heart and soul of scholarship is to listen carefully to many people with diverse views and to read as many books and articles as possible with differing approaches and conclusions about the same topic. Then, he said, you must carefully and thoroughly think through the material for yourself. Only then may you write it down and take responsibility for what you yourself think and say.

That priest's advice seemed quite reasonable, and the class was clearly processing the possibilities inherent in his statement. Before we young scholars got too far in our thinking, however, the wise man paused and, with a mischievous and knowing smile, he bellowed, "Remember, dear students, if you copy from one source, that's plagiarism; if you copy from many sources, that's scholarship!"

I have taken my old professor's advice to heart whenever I research a particular topic. I have learned the importance of utilizing only accurate information. Any researcher soon discovers that just because something appears in one place does not mean that it is valid or true or necessarily reliable. As you read this book, you can be confident that I have carefully verified as much as possible the facts and information that I use from multiple sources.

I was especially concerned that I rely on accurate information because the topic of this book is of great importance to me personally. I love the Catholic

Church and have always been thoroughly committed to it to this day. Intimately associated to that commitment is my life in Catholic education. I have been honored to serve as a De LaSalle Brother for more than four decades of my life and have been involved in Catholic education the entire time.

So I have read, listened, discussed, argued, and thought about the topics discussed here. I have felt it especially important to assure the validity of my conclusions and have sought views and opinions that challenged my preliminary conclusions to assure that they were not simply my personal biases. I have "copied" ideas and thoughts from many, many sources. However, for their integration into my own conclusions, I take full responsibility.

In order to make this book more approachable and readable to a wider audience, I do not treat the subject matter in the style of a formalized, academic research structure. Be assured, though, that while it is my intention that this work be accessible to all I do not want the rigor of the thoughts, ideas, and observations expressed herein to be compromised. If you want to criticize my conclusions, that is your prerogative; but please do not conclude that I don't know what I'm talking about just because I have chosen not to cite every source of every fact or idea in the book. I'll leave that task to another book, by me or by someone else. It is the conclusions that are the important thing here, because it is the conclusions that must lead to action sooner rather than later.

Despite my intention for clarity and readability, however, this book is not conducive to a quick speed-reading. Because of the nature of this subject matter that involves the church situated in a new global society of the third millennium, careful consideration must be given to distinctions, complexities, and nuanced statements.

At the Vatican's Apostolic Palace in Rome are many magnificent works of art for all to see and appreciate. One in particular holds a special place in my heart and psyche. There are, of course, many works of art that the world may judge as superior to this particular one, but we all know that art becomes meaningful to individuals for reasons that others may not grasp. In this case, because of the particular meaning this work has for me, it has taken on an exceptional significance in terms of this book.

On the wall of the *Stanza della Signatura* is Raphael's High Renaissance fresco masterpiece titled, "The School of Athens." In this fresco, standing and sitting in a magnificently appointed classical Greek study area are many of the philosophers of that time. Central in this fresco are Plato and Aristotle in conversation. Plato is clearly depicted as an old, wise, grey-bearded, barefooted man, while Aristotle is envisioned as a young, striking, well-dressed man. Plato's arm is raised, with a finger pointing up as if he were bringing "the heavens" to the attention of his young student. Aristotle, alongside but just slightly ahead of Plato, has his arm and hand extended and outstretched on a horizontal plane as if to remind Plato that they are presently on this earth and not in the heavens—"And, Plato, don't you forget it," he seems to be telling his master.

Experts may not see exactly what I see in this painting; but most agree that Plato is pointing toward the heavens because he is the more theoretical and esoteric philosopher. Aristotle, on the other hand, is the empirical and forward-looking philosopher who emphasizes real, daily, concrete, worldly particulars.

For me, it is most fitting that this fresco is in a place of prominence in the Vatican. Actually, I believe it should be placed in a main entrance to the Vatican City State for all to see as they enter. We are told that a picture is worth a thousand words. But for me this fresco reveals so much more than a thousand words: It is a multi-volume "book" that can stand on its own as an insightful and poignant treatise on the situation in which the institutional church finds itself today. The faithful—and the not so faithful—are continuously and forcefully reminding those leading the institutional church that their actions and manner of administration leave much to be desired. (To be clear, I know the church is both a human and divine entity, with human actors and divine grace interacting. When I use the term institutional church I am referring to those human organizational structures and personnel within the church, the persons and structures that serve the rest of the church as leaders and middle-managers. It includes the organization of the Vatican and all the dioceses throughout the world.)

I make no supposition that a solution to the issues I raise here will necessarily be found. In fact, I believe that there is a case to be made that no simple solution is possible. The institutional church is presently being confronted with multifaceted, complex, and diverse situations and scandals. There is a widely perceived, seemingly intractable institutional culture that says "authority means never having to say we're wrong." The institutional church seems to be accepting change only in the sense that it believes it can deal with reality by means of some new public relations tactics and superficial organizational (or even liturgical language) changes. This, however, is not going to work. Complete transformation is what is required.

Transformation as a dynamic force, both organizationally and spiritually, requires that the institutional church begin to see for itself—and do for itself—what it does not now see or do. The institutional church must become more open, more transparent, more accepting of diversity, and—this is the toughest one—more democratic.

I set out my case for arriving at this conclusion, knowing full well that in the church, just as in Raphael's "The School of Athens," there necessarily is need to point a finger toward the heavens while concurrently serving the needs of the world. Difficult to do? Yes. But, that is what the Incarnation is all about.

The institutional church must become more open, more transparent, more accepting of diversity, and more democratic.

Transformation is always difficult, and there will always be those who resist efforts to do things differently. However, it is important for all of us to understand the basic qualities essential to being responsive to the here and now. In this regard, it is good to heed the advice of Benjamin Franklin. In his *Poor Richard's Almanac*, he observed that "Experience holds a dear school, but only a fool will learn no other way." It is my hope that the church will embrace the "here and now" and live in a new emerging world. We need not to recreate the past but rather to invent a future that makes the Gospel alive once again in the world.

Because this book is an attempt to make clear what is so complex and necessarily filled with ambiguity, I have kept each chapter brief and offer an elaboration of a single focused point in each segment. I also incorporate many ideas from presentations that I have given and from my other written works over the years, because they have given rise to my present conclusions. Actually, I am well aware that each chapter could very well be expanded into a book unto itself, especially if the aim of the book were to present the matter as a structured academic research study. It is my hope that if anyone finds merit in the topics that I address in each chapter they will take these ideas and study them further. That is the true nature of intellectual inquiry.

The Holy Spirit is alive and well and speaking through many good people in the church. It is time for us to have the courage to be open and listen to one another, even those whose understandings may be different than our own. The constantly shrinking globe is bringing different people, different cultures, and different religions together. That sounds wonderfully positive to me. However, instead of this global phenomenon bringing peace and love to the world, we see much intolerance, marginalization, and, yes, even terrorism. We in the church, too, can quickly close off discussion and sharing of different ideas. But that would be a disaster, for we truly do have a quandary in the institutional church today; it is a quandary that desperately needs unraveling. This book is my contribution to that task.

Brother Louis DeThomasis, FSC
Rome, Italy
Lent 2012

CHAPTER 1

Is the Institutional Church Dying?

• • • • • •

Death is not the greatest loss in life.
The greatest loss is what dies inside us
while we live.

NORMAN COUSINS

• • • • • •

To even raise the question of whether or not the institutional church as we know it is "dying" is to be considered by some to be heresy.

It is not through disloyalty or with mean-spiritedness that I have come to feel compelled to ask this question. It is precisely because of my faithfulness to the church and my conviction that the Good News of Jesus Christ is for all humankind that I am driven, at this late point in my own life, not only to attempt to answer this frightful question but, more importantly, to begin to seek a solution to the consequences of whatever answer may arise.

I am a 70-year-old De LaSalle Brother, entering my eighth decade of life with anticipation, appropriate energy, and some well-developed understandings about the church that I feel I have not only a right but a duty to present to whomever might want to listen.

What sort of positive or negative bias about the church has made you want to read a book that asks this volatile question? The "institution" spoken of here may be the church of which you have felt part of all your life and love as much as I do. Or, perhaps, you once were a member of this church and, for any number of reasons, have chosen to reject or simply ignore it. You might well be a member of the clergy, a professed religious, a bishop, a cardinal, or the current or future pope. You could work for the church in some capacity, or you may have a job and a family and are involved in civic and community affairs as "just" a layperson. You might even be one of our non-Roman-Catholic Christian brethren, or the follower of another faith, or someone with no faith at all that wants to see what the big hubbub is all about inside the Catholic Church today.

It doesn't matter to me, because these thoughts are for everyone, regardless of where one stands or sits *vis-a-vis* Catholicism. It is important to me, however, that every reader come to the realization that for me to constructively criticize something I love with accuracy and fairness I must also clearly acknowledge that I am a sinner myself. Indeed, it is only with age, reflection, and prayer that I have been able to muster the courage to discuss the problems, transgressions, mistakes, and sins of the church, because I know that I am as guilty as anyone of many of the sins decried in this book. I too have been insensitive, closed-minded, arrogant, self-centered, too-quick-to-defend-the-indefensible, overly protective of myself and my fellow church-members. For this I am sorry. And for this reason I offer this book as a small token of atonement.

I believe that the death of the institutional church as we all know it can be the last opportunity for it to transform itself into something that once again is able to carry out its original purpose.

On the other hand, because of my lifetime commitment to the church, I can claim a certain amount of expertise on this subject. If you know me, you will agree; if you do not, I hope this book will demonstrate to you that I have developed some appropriate knowledge and insight on the subject of Catholicism.

Is the institutional church dying? Yes. And even though it may be politic to add "unfortunately," I offer no such qualification. I believe that the death of the institutional church as we all know it can be the last opportunity for it to transform itself into something that once again is able to carry out its original purpose.

An explanation of what I mean is certainly in order.

First, the "institutional church" needs to be defined as it is used here. Specifically, my thoughts are about only one part of the Roman Catholic Church: the structural part. The "institutional church" is not the Catholic people throughout the world who attend Mass, who do good works, who relate almost exclusively in terms of their faith to their local parish. Nor is the institutional church the divinely inspired mystery of the "communion" of the People of God in unity with one another today and with the long line of followers of Jesus Christ that went before us and will follow us. The institutional church, as it is commonly understood and appears to the public, is the formal structural hierarchy within the Vatican and, by extension, the local churches throughout the world within the office of each duly appointed Roman Catholic bishop.

Second, the entire church, much less the narrower institutional church, is not the kingdom of God. In Vatican II's "Dogmatic Constitution on the Church" (*Lumen Gentium*) there is a significant passage that says:

> From this source the Church, equipped with the gifts of its Founder and faithfully guarding His precepts of charity, humility, and self-sacrifice, receives the mission to proclaim and to spread among all peoples the Kingdom of Christ and of God and to be, on earth, the initial budding forth of the Kingdom. (LG 5)

In other words, according to Vatican II, which is the "institutional church" speaking at its most united and powerful, the church may be a "means" to the Kingdom, but it is not the Kingdom. At its best, it is "the initial budding forth of the Kingdom."

Third, the church, as it is lived by Catholics each day, is the "People of God." It is faithful, dynamic, and true to the Gospel of Jesus Christ. The church as the People of God lives on and thrives in this world because Jesus never stops bestowing his grace and spirit: "I have come that they may have life, and have it abundantly" (John 10:10). Throughout the world can be seen lay women and men, consecrated religious women and men, priests, bishops, cardinals, and popes who make real the love of Christ through the abundance of work and sacrifice they offer to the poor, the needy, and the marginalized. These are the people who make real what the church must be, who make real the words attributed to St. Teresa of Avila:

> Christ has no body now on earth but yours,
> no hands but yours,
> no feet but yours,
> yours are the eyes
> through which Christ's compassion is to look out to the earth,
> yours are the feet
> by which he is to go about doing good,
> and yours are the hands
> by which he is to bless us now.

Finally, an important distinction to keep in mind in approaching an understanding of the institutional church is the keen insight of the late Cardinal Avery Dulles, SJ. In his talks and writings he talked of the church not only in terms of the People of God and its institutional structures, but also as a mystical communion, a sacrament, a herald, and a servant. All these images and models are involved in our ongoing and evolving understanding of the church. Each traits mentioned by Dulles is necessary for a healthy and vibrant church.

Thus, the church is many things. Therefore, in a sense, to talk of the institutional nature of the church necessarily involves a certain amount of fragmentation of what in totality is the Catholic Church. But it must be done here so that specific aspects of the church today can be isolated and we can be appropriately critical where criticism is due. Therefore, it is proposed that throughout this book:

The *institutional church* referred to is that part of the Roman Catholic Church that involves the structures, infrastructures, administrative offices, rules, regulations, rituals, and the personnel—whether clerical or lay—that have evolved in the church over time. These outward organizational structures were developed not from the infallible processes that the Holy Spirit nourishes to protect the church from error but rather by the very human and fallible people who make up the church.

It is very important that this definition is clear. I have encountered very serious and faith-filled people who believe that my ideas amount to finding fault with the people in the pews or their priests. That is not the case at all. Nor is mine a criticism of particular local bishops and cardinals, except as they offer examples of what is wrong. They, too, are trying to respond to the Spirit, just as the wider group of the faithful are.

My critique of the institutional church is aimed at the public persona of the church itself, as observed in its structures and the people representing it (*de facto*, mostly clerics and therefore mostly men). It is the super-structure of the church, the one that makes the institutional rules and has made the institutional mistakes that have gotten us into our present situation. In no way am I even remotely questioning the entire church's faith-filled inner life of holiness and grace. The reader must keep this important distinction in mind so that the context of my critical observations is not seen as any kind of destructive attack on the church in general. It is the institutional church that is dying, not the church we Catholics belong to.

• • • • • •

Can the People of God continue to function with the present day institutional model of the church?

• • • • • •

And, given this situation, a significant question arises: Can the People of God continue to function with the present day institutional model of the church? The answer to that question is no.

"Is the institutional church dying?"

My answer is: "Yes, fortunately!"

It is fortunate because this death can be the occasion for a *metanoia* in the church. *Metanoia* is theologically understood to mean a change of mind and heart; within the church it would mean repentance that leads to and is an occasion for transformation.

Does the institutional church need repentance and transformation? It seems to me that the answer to this is incontrovertible. Here are some recent incidents and happenings around the world that directly involve the institutional church. They all occurred in the two years immediately before this book was written. These examples make clear the specific nature of how the institutional church has been conducting itself and why this gives rise to a call for its transformation. This list is not exhaustive, and many of the incidents are well known to the faithful. I offer them here as examples only, and while any one of them might have a "explanation" or a "legal response," the cumulative effect of them is to say that something is terribly wrong in the institutional church and needs to be radically changed.

November 2009—A 27-year-old woman pregnant with her fifth child went to the Catholic hospital in Phoenix, Arizona, with pulmonary hypertension and experiencing heart failure that would most likely be fatal to her if the pregnancy continued. Sister Margaret McBride, RSM, a well-respected Catholic hospital administrator, consulted thoroughly with the medical professionals and medical ethicists at the hospital regarding the likely result of allowing the pregnancy to continue and determined that it would mean the mother's death. The hospital group finally and under time constraints approved a procedure to save the patient, which resulted in the death of the fetus. Bishop Thomas Olmsted, the Catholic bishop of Phoenix, then announced to the public that Sister Margaret was excommunicated for officially permitting an "abortion." Local newspapers began to ask, "Why is it that priests who commit sexual abuse crimes against living children are not excommunicated, but Sister Margaret is?"

Easter Sunday Mass 2010—The former Vatican Secretary of State, Cardinal Angelo Sodano, with the Pope present and thousands of the faithful in attendance, characterized the media's coverage of clerical sex abuse as "petty gossip." As one would expect, the international media was fully present. After this talk, Benedict XVI embraced Cardinal Sodano in front of all at Saint Peter's Square.

Spring 2010—Cardinal Christoph Schonborn, Archbishop of Vienna, and a former student of Pope Benedict XVI, caused a major disturbance at the Vatican when he said that mandatory celibacy for priests should be in "unflinching examination" in the sex abuse scandals in the church. He also criticized his fellow prelate Cardinal Sodano for the comments he made about the media's sex abuse coverage of the church being "petty gossip." Then, according to the leading Catholic newspaper in Great Britain, *The Tablet*, and newspapers in Austria, Cardinal Schonborn charged that Cardinal Sodano had thwarted some of the Vatican's child abuse investigations, including confirmed child-abuse acts of the former archbishop of Vienna, Cardinal Hans Hermann Groer, a good friend of Pope John Paul II. (Also presumably thwarted was investigation of Father Marcial Maciel Degollado—founder of the Legion of Christ—who was guilty of many sexual abuse crimes.) Furthermore, Cardinal Schonborn said that the church should give more consideration to the quality of homosexual relationships, and that a stable same-sex relationship is better than a series of promiscuous relationships.

Cardinal Schonborn was summoned to the Vatican for some "clarification" of his remarks. Some Vatican *cognoscenti* describe this meeting as Schonborn being taken to the "Papal Woodshed." As one would expect, there was a communiqué issued as a result of this meeting in which Schonborn's unequivocal and clear comments were described as being misinterpreted by the media. What is most interesting is that Schonborn to date has issued no retraction of his comments.

May 2010—In Germany, Bishop Walter Mixa of Augsburg was accused of sexually abusing minors. He resigned. Three Irish bishops were criticized about how they handled sexual abuse cases within their jurisdiction. They resigned.

June 24, 2010—At 10:30 AM, at the Catholic Archbishopric of Mechelen-Brussels in Belgium, there was a monthly meeting of the episcopal conference, with the *papal nuncio* present. Without announcement or invitation, police and court officials entered the building and conducted a search, confiscating mobile phones and documents, and ordered that no one could leave the building. This situation lasted until about 7:30 PM.

All present were interrogated concerning sexual abuse within the territory of the archdiocese. Additionally, Belgian legal authorities actually invaded tombs of deceased archbishops in search of possible hidden documents. Also, police raided the home of the retired archbishop of Brussels, Cardinal Godfried Danneels, and confiscated his computer and various documents.

June 2010—The Supreme Court of the United States of America (with then five of the nine Justices being Catholic) ruled that it would permit a sex abuse lawsuit in the state of Oregon to proceed against the Vatican, a recognized sovereignty.

June 2010—Media reports the growing credibility of claims of financial corruption by Cardinal Crescenzio Sepe when he was head from 2001-2006 of the Vatican's department *Propaganda Fide*, which controls very large real estate holdings that reportedly earn about 56 million Euro per year. Cardinal Sepe is now the Archbishop of Naples, and magistrates there want to question him about his alleged serious illegal financial activities.

January 2011—The Associated Press reported (January 19, 2011) on a 1997 letter marked "strictly confidential" sent by the Vatican's diplomat to Ireland, Archbishop Luciano Storero, to the Irish bishops telling them not to report all suspected child-abuse cases to police. This document points in essence to the Vatican's rejection of a 1996 Irish church initiative to help the police identify pedophile priests. Critics say that this letter clearly undermines persistent Vatican claims that

Rome never instructed bishops to withhold evidence or suspicion of these crimes from police authorities. The A.P. report went on to state, "Child-abuse activists in Ireland said the 1977 letter demonstrates that the protection of pedophile priests from criminal investigation was not only sanctioned by Vatican leaders but also ordered by them."

February 2011—Just five years since a previous Philadelphia, Pennsylvania, grand jury exposed the molestation of hundreds of children by 63 archdiocesan priests, a new 124-page grand jury final document charges additional and current sexual abuse cases. These incidents occurred after all the apologies and assurances from archdiocesan officials with their promises of no more cover-ups and supposed strict "no tolerance" policies regarding sexual abuse of minors. Yet there were 37 priests still active in archdiocesan ministry despite credible allegations against them. For the first time in the pedophilia crisis in the U.S. there was also a criminal indictment of an archdiocesan official not accused of pedophilia. Msgr. William Lynn (episcopal vicar staffing the chancery from 1992 to 2004) was charged with two felonies for endangering the welfare of a minor and for attempting to cover up those crimes. An editorial in the Philadelphia *Inquirer* (February 17, 2007) said that although many were willing to give church officials a second chance, this new grand jury report "...shows that many of the reforms appear to have been designed to protect the church rather than victims. Worse, the cover-up continues and allegedly reaches to top officials."

Given this exposition of these additional recent cover-ups, the Archdiocese of Philadelphia was compelled by public pressure to place 21 of the 37 accused priests on "administrative leave" until their cases are properly investigated. This is the largest single group suspension of priests in the history of the church in the United States. The archdiocese did not disclose the names of those priests. This omission caused more outcries from the public concerning the church's continued lack of understanding as to how such credible accusations must be treated in order to protect children from such abuse.

May 2, 2011—In an official statement the Vatican stated that "The Holy Father, Pope Benedict XVI, has relieved His Excellency Msgr. William M. Morris of the pastoral care of the Diocese of Toowoomba," which is in Australia. Bishop Morris was ousted after Pope Benedict appointed U.S. Archbishop Charles J. Chaput of Denver to conduct an apostolic visitation of the Diocese of Toowoomba. Archbishop Chaput's report was not made public; however, a pastoral letter that Bishop Morris sent out to the people of the diocese five years ago was the apparent reason for this dismissal. In that letter he had raised the issue of ordaining women and married people as a possible remedy to the dire priest shortage experienced in the diocese. Archbishop John Bathersby of Brisbane said that the treatment of Bishop Morris is the way the church now operates and that it is sad it has come to this.

June 2011—A movement of Viennese priests called "Initiative of Parish Priests" publicly proclaimed a "Call to Disobedience." These priests are calling for significant reforms in the church. In fact, a report in the *National Catholic Reporter* (July 12, 2011) titled "300 Austrian Clerics Call for Women Priests, Reform" states that, "The initiative, which says it has more than 300 members, suggested saying a public prayer at every Mass for church reform; giving Communion to everyone who approaches the altar in good faith, including divorced Catholics who have remarried without an annulment; allowing women to preach at Mass; and supporting the ordination of women and married men."

July 2011—Irish Prime Minister Enda Kenny, referring to a judicial investigation of clergy sexual abuse in the Diocese of Cloyne during a parliamentary session, described the Vatican's actions in its handling of the situation as dominated by "dysfunction," "elitism," and "narcissism." He went on further to tell the Vatican that it should be penitent for the "horrors" it caused as a result of its hiding and denials of the abuse.

Sexual abuse, corruption, authoritarianism, lack of transparency, and cover-ups have all been collapsing into and on top of the institutional church. It does not matter whether one is liberal or conservative, orthodox or unorthodox, believer or non-believer. One cannot help but be amazed that the prestige, reverence, and esteem that once belonged to the institutional church and its leaders are no longer there. The "tipping point" has been reached, and the moral authority, honor, and respect that the institutional church once elicited from most peoples and secular institutions around the globe simply no longer exists.

In fact, this loss of moral and legitimate authority in the conduct and *modus operandi* of the institutional church has been directly caused by its inability to admit it can be wrong. The institutional church cannot (and should not) blame anyone but itself. Too often it has acted in a manner that made people believe it has tried to protect its own image more than fulfill its sacred duty to protect people, especially children.

• • • • • •

If there is metanoia and transformation from within, then there can and will be "resurrection" for the institutional church.

• • • • • •

It is not the press, media, or "anti-Catholics" that have caused this travesty in the church. Oh, indeed, they were all there, eager to report the mess with much glee. But it was the institutional church that gave them the ammunition. And if the institutional church continues to ignore its responsibility and culpability, and if it does not show real and true repentance by effectively transforming itself, then the dying process will culminate in a complete death sentence in the not-too-distant future.

However, if there is *metanoia* and transformation from within, then there can and will be "resurrection" for the institutional church. Granted, this is a big "if."

The *National Catholic Reporter's* John L. Allen, a consummate and longtime Vatican-watcher, published his take on what he described as "...the torrent of big-ticket Vatican stories…that shook the Vatican." He believes that this deluge of bad news stories similar to the ones mentioned previously "…symbolize and advance the collapse of Catholicism as a culture-shaping majority in the West." Allen observes that taken together all these transgressions and lack of transparency reported about the Vatican and dioceses "…suggest that the final pillars of deference by civil authorities to the Catholic Church are crumbling." Then he goes on to opine that "…not just religion's cultured despisers, but many Catholics themselves, welcome all this, seeing it as a long-overdue dose of humility and accountability."

Allen observes that it is clear that Pope Benedict XVI knows that the church in the West will surely be in the minority but that Benedict believes it will be a "creative minority." This term reflects the words of philosopher Arnold Toynbee who espoused "… when great civilizations enter a crisis, they either decay or are renewed from within by 'creative minorities' who offer a compelling vision of the future."

But who will be the "creative minorities" within the Catholic Church who can restore the legitimacy of the institutional church? That is the real question. And that is the quandary this book will attempt to unravel.

CHAPTER 2

The Subversion of Vatican II

• • • • • •

May we never confuse honest dissent
with disloyal subversion.

DWIGHT DAVID EISENHOWER

• • • • • •

In more than thirty years serving in Catholic education, both on the second-ary and university levels, I have seen the Catholic Church lose many gen-erous young people because the institutional leaders do not give them the "spiritual space" (this will be discussed further in a later chapter) to question, to dialogue, to doubt, to challenge. In fact, some of these institutional leaders contend (often behind closed doors) that the church is better off without these querulous youth and instead shower their attention on young people who ac-cept the church with docility and are supposedly "flocking" into the church. It is not the young people (and many of their parents) who are leaving the church who are the supposed "cafeteria Catholics," however. It is those who are picking and choosing from the teachings of Vatican II as if it were not as "legitimate" a Council of the entire church as, say, Vatican I or even Trent.

There is a certain humorous story that has been circulating around Rome—in certain circles—that has a particularly biting message. One fine day in paradise, the Holy Trinity was sitting around reminiscing about some pleas-ant places they had visited on earth. The Father said to the other Two, "I really would like to re-visit Mount Sinai. I have many fond memories of my encoun-ter there with Moses." Then Jesus jumped into the conversation and said, "You know, come to think of it, I would really enjoy going back to Nazareth for a brief visit. I have wonderful memories of my childhood there with my loving parents, Mary and Joseph." Then they both turned to the Holy Spirit, but the Spirit was silent and pensive. So they asked, "Holy Spirit, isn't there some place on earth that you would like to revisit?" After some hesitation the Holy Spirit answered, "Well, I would like to visit Rome. I have heard so much about it, but I've never really been there!"

When anyone reviews the litany of recent church scandals, missteps, mistakes, and public relation blunders, must that person—the faithful, the not-so-faithful, or the unfaithful—not stop a moment and ask, "Is the Holy Spirit really guiding the church today?"

My answer is: of course! Probably never before in the history of the church—given these incredible happenings—has there been greater *de facto* evidence of the grace-filled presence of the Holy Spirit. (I'll explain this in a minute.) But (and this is a big but), surely the amateurish solutions proffered by the institutional church in response to the current crisis could lead anyone with a modicum of common sense to question the presence of the Holy Spirit in Rome or in most chancery offices today,

Yet the Holy Spirit dwells, as always, in the hearts and minds of the faithful—the lay people, the vowed religious, the priests and deacons, the prelates and popes. We Catholics know that when we all come together as church in a collegial and faith-filled spirit that God—in the Person of the Holy Spirit—is there in our midst. This is actually a key teaching of the church, part of its much misunderstood and often misused "*magisterium.*"

However, as evidenced by the concrete actions of the institutional church leaders recently, one should be able to admit that it is not, even on the face of it, the Vatican curia or bureaucracy that is the fullness of the teaching authority of the church. *De facto*, though, the present crew seems to act as if they were. It is not disloyalty, meanness, or even impoliteness to point out this truth. It is more like the young boy who cried out in the children's story, "But the Emperor has no clothes!"

It is precisely their very faith in the Catholic Church that compels the People of God to acknowledge this reality. Charles P. Pierce, a Boston *Globe* magazine writer and *NPR* contributor, seems to represent the views of many Catholics today, who more and more are coming to the realization that the bureaucracy of the Vatican is not the authority vested with the solemn authority of infallibility.

Pierce notes that a fundamental rule of his Catholicism is that "nobody gets to tell me I'm not Catholic." He goes on to declare:

> Many Catholics are out of patience with intramural church solutions that seem to do little more than push the cases down the road and keep in place the sclerotic institutional structure and the paranoid mania for secrecy that allowed the corruption to flourish in the first place.

Of course, when these kinds of observations are made, they can easily be dismissed as simple acrimony on the part of a single commentator. This is called "shooting the messenger." As to the recipients of such criticism—the institutional church—its leaders can get quite defensive and start squelching the criticism through the use of authoritative sanctions, including excommunication. Here is what is happening in Rome today: Many church insiders, as they increasingly feel themselves under siege, are now saying that the church will have to get smaller and only allow the "true" and "faithful" (in their minds) followers of Jesus Christ to remain. This type of argument does not come from the Holy Spirit. It is simply the old institutional self-preservation argument of "quality" over "quantity." Of course, the rest of us may be justified by observing that such an argument is really an excuse for not being willing to change the way institutions do things. In order for *metanoia*, a spiritual reawakening, to take place in the institutional church today, this argument is going to have to be taken head on and revealed for what it is.

Change is hard for an individual to accomplish and even more traumatic

The bureaucracy of the Vatican is not the authority vested with the solemn authority of infallibility.

for an institution that has many individuals within its structures with vested interests in the status quo to protect. Yet the reason we have a theology of *meta-noia* in the Catholic Church in the first place is because many of our church fathers and mothers and holy prophets knew it would take the Holy Spirit to transform us, not only as individuals but also as the institutional church. Transforming man-made, fallible structures and organizations is a meaningful task, but it takes the Holy Spirit to pour grace, zeal, and wisdom into the hearts of individuals like you and me so that we will speak up—yes, with insistent, faith-filled force but also with sensitive, caring, and loving actions toward the institutional church itself.

An example of this kind of Spirit-driven voice was exhibited poignantly and strikingly by a much better source than I will ever be: a sensitive, prophetic, and caring man within the institutional church who knows the system from the inside out. The person to whom I refer is retired Bishop Kevin Dowling of Rustenburgh, South Africa. On June 1, 2010, Bishop Dowling gave a presentation to a group of influential lay Catholics in Cape Town regarding his view of the current state of the church. He presumed that since this was a private gathering, no media would be present. However, a reporter did infiltrate the gathering, and Bishop Dowling's "off the record" talk quickly became public. The *National Catholic Reporter* called the Bishop about this, and he gave a copy of his talk to *NCR* with permission to publish the text.

To set the context of his presentation, Bishop Dowling began by relating what took place in April, 2010, at the Basilica of the National Shrine of the Immaculate Conception in Washington, D.C. Bishop Edward Slattery celebrated a Mass in Latin. He wore the 20-yard-long, bright-red flowing train called the *cappa magna*—a clear symbol of the *Tridentine* Mass. Bishop Dowling stated, "For me, such a display of what amounts to triumphalism in a church torn apart by the sexual abuse scandal is most unfortunate. What happened there bore the marks of a medieval royal court, not the humble, servant leadership modeled by Jesus."

It seems bizarre to me that the systems and structures within the institutional church did not consider the adverse public reaction that such a "show" would cause. After all, is there really a good reason to flaunt such a symbol in a church that professes a "preferential option for the poor"? Does the *cappa magna* on a bishop, in all its brilliant, regal color, really reflect the Christ whom the priest represents at Mass?

In actuality, this regal manifestation and the many other blunders that have already been mentioned indicate that, even assuming good will and good intentions (which is sometimes a stretch to do), there are many in the institutional church's power structures today that just don't get it! Again, Bishop Dowling presents a keen insight into this aberrant behavior. He believes that since the pontificate of John Paul II, and continuing with Benedict XVI, there has been an attitude of "restorationism" taking place. He bluntly states that such behavior occurs:

• • • • • •

The institutional church seems to be doing all that it can to negate the results of its own most recent ecumenical council.

• • • • • •

...in order to 'restore' a previous, or more controllable, model of church through an increasingly centralized power structure; a structure which now controls everything in the life of the church through a network of Vatican congregations led by cardinals who ensure strict compliance with what is deemed by them to be "orthodox." Those who do not comply face censure and punishment, e.g., theologians who are forbidden to teach in Catholic faculties.

What is so very strange and inconsistent is that the institutional church, which defends its role as protector of the faith and as conveyor of the truth as decreed by the *magisterium* of the church, seems to be doing all that it can to negate the results of its own most recent ecumenical council, Vatican II.

Have they forgotten that Pope John XXIII—as much the Vicar of Christ on Earth as Popes John Paul II and Benedict XVI—convened the college of bishops from all over the world to join with the bishop of Rome to exercise its teaching authority with the assurance that such collegiality is imbued with the presence of the Holy Spirit? Or, as Bishop Dowling said of Vatican II, "...its vision, its principles, and the direction it gave are to be followed and implemented by all, from the pope to the peasant farmer in the fields of Honduras."

Instead of fostering and teaching the wisdom of that great collegial body of the church, Pope Benedict XVI now espouses in his own words a "hermeneutic of continuity." Now, biblical hermeneutics involves the interpretation of the books of the Bible in order that the meaning of what is communicated is understandable in today's culture. It attempts to explain the principles and genuine sense of the Bible. But the Pope now seems to be presenting conservatives inside the institutional church with an intellectual and theological platform that skews the very essence of Vatican II into something less than a new and developing revelation of that collegial body. Instead, his personal characterization of the Council within a context of a "hermeneutic of continuity" emphasizes that Vatican II *in no way*(!) transformed earlier teachings of the church and its traditions. Of course, this distinction made by the Pope, a great theological scholar in his own right, is patient in his precise intellectual nomenclature; however, even with that papal caveat one does not have to be even a mediocre scholar to understand probably his true view about Vatican II is that it really didn't change much in the church.

It is vitally important in the life of the church to point out this distinction between the new views proclaimed by Vatican II and Pope Benedict's interpretations of such pronouncements. Even the casual observer sees the growing tensions that arise between the various factions in the church today. One sees antagonistic camps of "liberals" vs. "conservatives," "orthodox" vs. "revisionists," and "the faithful" vs. "the heretics." Mean-spiritedness, hostility, and acrimony flourish in a church that should be all about the peace and love that Jesus brought to our world. Certainly, all sides are to blame as we permit these differences to obfuscate the "Good News" of the faith.

Yet now, more than ever, those of us who believe in the vision of Vatican II cannot back down from speaking the truth as we see it. The institutional church needs to respond in a vitally new and more effective way to Vatican II, one that will allow the church to once more "teach as Jesus did." However, to turn once again to the "insider" with first-hand knowledge, note the words of Bishop Dowling:

Since Vatican II there has been no such similar exercise of teaching authority by the *magisterium*. Instead, there have been a series of decrees, pronouncements, and decisions that have been given various labels stating, for example, that they must be firmly held to with "internal assent" by the Catholic faithful, but in reality they are simply the theological or pastoral interpretations or opinions of those who have power at the center of the church. They have not been solemnly defined as belonging to the "deposit of the faith" to be believed and followed, therefore, by all Catholics, as with other solemnly proclaimed dogmas. For example, the issues of celibacy for the priesthood and the ordination of women have been withdrawn even from the realm of discussion. Therefore, such pronouncements are open to scrutiny—to discern whether they are in accord, for example, with the fundamental theological vision of Vatican II, or whether there is, indeed, a case to be made for a different interpretation or opinion.

I want to say that a strident, fundamentalist, "one shoe fits all" church is not the church of the People of God. The awesome and urgent need for *metanoia* and transformation within the institutional church is clearly evident. The Catholic Church must be a humble, inclusive, teaching (in the best sense of that word) church. Jesus' command to "Go and teach all nations" is not in any way a qualified statement. It is meant for all of his followers for all time to all people.

CHAPTER 3

Is Our Critique Unfair, Overblown, Unnecessary?

• • • • • •

*Unkind criticism is never part
of a meaningful critique of you.
Its purpose is not to teach or to help,
its purpose is to punish.*

BARBARA SHER

• • • • • •

It is very easy to sit on the sidelines and criticize anything or anyone, from one's favorite sports team, to politicians, to the restaurant that used to be good but now is only adequate. For some people, criticism of the institutional church is an enjoyable activity, almost a sport. "You no playa the game; you no maka the rules" is an old saying that captures much of the Catholic world's attitude toward Rome.

It can be an almost pleasant experience to see others offering the institutional church minor criticism one heartily endorses. I experience this myself. And when that favorite criticism becomes a particularly popular topic in the press and media, it can be a near delight. However, when the criticism of the church we love is associated with allegations of real impropriety, serious mistakes, or even criminal behavior, there needs to be a distinctly qualitative difference in the impact and *gravitas* of our critique.

Of course, the ability to accept criticism varies with different institutions, and the Roman Catholic Church is one of the worst at accepting, much less learning from, it. If we criticize the institutional church's individuals, structures, policies, or even non-*magisterium* doctrines, the onus is on us to prove that we are operating in good faith, and we will have to live with the possibility of falling under suspicion of disloyalty or being accused of some sort of treachery. The church has clearly been persecuted by governments, anti-Catholics, and those of other and no religious beliefs throughout its history. It has a right to be gun-shy.

In times past, there certainly were critics of the church who were people of ill will, malcontents, antagonists, mean-spirited or way-out fringe liberals or conservatives. Complicating matters now, however, is that for better and for worse many of us who are critics of our institutional church leaders are mature, often well-educated adults who have lived our entire lives as faithful, church-going, even traditional Catholics. And now we simply cannot understand how the institutional church has fallen so far and so quickly in our eyes and in the eyes of so many outside the church.

We do not see in the male-dominated power structures of the institutional church anyone willing to understand the real life struggles of the People of God.

Additionally, younger Catholics are becoming more critical because they do not see in the male-dominated power structures of the institutional church anyone willing to understand the real life struggles of the People of God, including issues of human sexuality, women's roles in today's globalized society and church, and the need for a deeper, more modern sense of servant leadership.

Meanwhile, many of these young people within the church seek a more expansive acceptance of a spirituality that is less concerned with rote formulas and rubrics and more embracing of the magnificent and enriching diversity that can be a legitimate and meaningful expression of the love they have for Jesus and for one another.

There is a "key" to this quandary that might help us unravel it. In 2006, astute business journalist Neil St. Anthony and I co-authored a book called *Doing Right in a Shrinking World*. This work identified "ideology" as the main culprit in modern business strategies to "do" ethics as though it were some kind of an overlay, like a new business slogan.

There seems to be the same problem inside the institutional church with ideology—or more precisely, with "ideologues," the executors of the ideology—that is the root cause of most of our problems in transforming the church. It is these ideologues within the power structure of the institutional church who have taken to expressing their particular ideological slant and opinions by stating them as pronouncements that require what they call "internal assent" by the faithful. No dialogue is allowed. No questions may be raised. "Take it or leave" (sic) seems to be the basic message. (And certainly a large number of Catholics have taken that message to heart—not just "marginal" Catholics but many who have been active all their lives are moving to other denominations or religions in droves. This is another part of the story that is being denied or ignored in Rome.)

Such insistence on "orthodoxy," or doctrinal agreement, may be at the heart of the unfortunate circumstances extant in today's church. Faithful Catholics can and do think for themselves and certainly no longer view docility and acquiescence to church officials as a requirement for faith. This is especially true when the purveyors of the ideology, by their action or inaction, have lost any claim to legitimate authority, which is the case in the Catholic Church today.

What is ideology? Simply stated, ideology is a systematic body of concepts, integrated assertions, and theories that constitute a view of reality. For some intellectuals, ideology appears much as it did in the times of the Enlightenment, which produced a set of "mechanical laws" to explain human nature. Today's ideologues, whether in academia, government, business, or the church, assimilate into their world-view a way of thinking and acting that is so rigid that decisions and judgments become almost "mechanistic" and insensitive to interpersonal dynamics.

Kenneth Minogue magnificently elaborates a thorough and insightful elaboration of the ideological approach to reality in his book, *Alien Powers: The Pure Theory of Ideology*. For Minogue, ideology is actually a perversion of reason, since it encourages its adherents to a tendency towards absolute certainty. Simply stated, they are right because they are the ones who said they are right. It can be said that ideology is to reason as gluttony is to fine dining, and as such the inevitable result is that ideology becomes what some have described as an "intellectual chameleon," since it can appear sometimes as a science, other times as a philosophy, and sometimes—and most dangerously—as religion.

There is a sarcastic dictum in the Vatican, *Roma locuta. Causa finita!*: "Rome has spoken. The question is closed!" That premise seems to indelicately characterize the propensity of not only the Catholic institutional church but any church or religion for that matter to think it needs to have all the answers and to end any dialogue generated among religionist followers. We can see this happening among some radical followers of Islam today. Why can we not see it when it happens in the institutional Catholic Church?

• • • • • •

Religious ideologues do nothing but stifle the human imagination in its quest to embrace the faith mystery.

• • • • • •

Religious ideologues do nothing but stifle the human imagination in its quest to embrace the faith mystery. It reduces the religion to neat, ideological formulae under the guise of "truth," "orthodoxy," "rules," and "doctrine." Is this not what Jesus fought against his entire life?

And what happens when the ideologues are men, and only men, and men so very thoroughly in charge? When men get control of any organization, watch out. I will address this point later when I discuss the need for the church to ordain women. (The recent sexual scandals and subsequent cover-up at the Athletic Department of Penn State University in Pennsylvania were noted by many commentators to have many parallels with what happened in the Catholic Church, not the least of which was that there were no women to be found anywhere in the power structure of each organization.)

In the church, there is an additional overlay of power because of the divine origin of the church itself. However, even this belief in the ultimate holiness and faithfulness of the church does not extend to the institutional leaders and organizational structures. There is simply too much history—from the Crusades to the Inquisition to the sale of indulgences to the persecution of Galileo to the pedophilia cover-up—to argue otherwise.

An important signal indicating that ideology is overshadowing the church's ability to proclaim the "Good News" is the feeling that there is currently a proliferation of laws, rules, rubrics, regulations, and excommunications coming out of Rome. After all, Cicero warned us some two thousand years ago—*Maximum Jus: Maxima Iniuria!*: The more law, the more injustice! It was Lord Acton, a lay Catholic in England, who wrote in 1870:

> I cannot accept your canon that we are to judge Pope and King unlike other men, with a favorable presumption that they did no wrong. If there is any presumption it is the other way, against the holders of power, increasing as the power increases. Historic responsibility has to make up for the want of legal responsibility. Power tends to corrupt, and absolute power corrupts absolutely. Great men are almost always bad men, even when they exercise influence and not authority, still more when you add the tendency or the certainty of corruption by authority. There is no worse heresy than that the office sanctifies the holder of it.

Even assuming the best intentions, care, and concern on the part of those who today comprise the institutional church, people perceive a rigidness, even a callousness, on the part of those in power in the church today. They seem to act like unaccountable "bosses" of the church who are attempting to impose their interpretation of reality on everyone—Catholic and non-Catholic alike. This makes them incapable of achieving a more multi-faceted and complex grasp of the real-life situation of most people. In fact, this developing, negative, pervasive tension has contributed to the coinage of the term "Taliban Catholicism" by John Allen of the *National Catholic Reporter*. The anger that has developed from this perceived state of affairs has become nasty and destructive to the church.

Because of this perception, there is a sustained criticism of the church as a whole that does not go away. People ask, "Why do you stay in a church that is so out of touch?" My answer is that the church is not the institutional church. The church is something greater, more permanent, more important, more loving, more relevant, more needed than what is going on in Rome right now. It is my job—and the job of other Catholics who love the church—to speak out and to demand (yes, that is the word) that the institutional church transform itself. If it does not, it will continue to die and will be replaced eventually by something else by the People of God.

When any ideology takes over in the power structures of any organization, it is no surprise that critics, even constructive ones, are viewed as anti-organization. Thus, critics of ideological tendencies within the Catholic Church are seen as anti-church. Then, a "systemic" defensive posture takes hold, and what suffers are subsidiarity, collegiality, personal responsibility, and individual rights. In essence, however, many of us do not see our honest and candid criticism of the institutional church as disloyal or unfair.

Still not convinced? Consider this. The growing criticism of the institutional church's conduct should not come as a surprise, given the evolution of how people have come to view the role of all institutions, including religious ones. A fine overview of these changes can be seen in *Modernization, Cultural Change, and Democracy* by Ronald Inglehart and Christian Welzel.

For the last three hundred years since the Industrial Revolution, the basic organizational values were simply these: bureaucratization, hierarchy, centralization of authority, and obedience to authority. Now, in our new, globalized society there has evolved a very different kind of dynamic within organizational entities. There is now a value on:

- decentralization of authority
- less bureaucracy
- less hierarchy
- greater participation of all in decision making
- an emphasis on individual autonomy, self-expression, and independent thinking
- no gender or racial or sexual-orientation discrimination.

How does the institutional church stack-up with these new traits and values? Is it any wonder that there is growing discontent among many faithful people?

Also, there is seen in today's more successful, appropriately performing institutions a much greater value placed on "feedback" from all stakeholders. The institutions that are functioning well establish effective processes to ensure that they are "hearing" and "seeing" what is "out there." These organizations initiate continuous assessment so that they are responsive and responsible to people outside their power structure. They promote self-assessment and self-correcting processes. And they make certain that their internal and external communications are open and clear.

Now consider: How does today's institutional church emulate and/or practice these values?

CHAPTER 4

Tradition and Reason:
The Way Out of the Quandary

• • • • • •

And who can doubt that it will lead to the worst disorders
when minds created free by God
are compelled to submit slavishly to an outside will?
When we are told to deny our senses
and subject them to the whim of others?

Galileo Galilei

• • • • • •

What is the way out of the quandary in which the church—both the People of God and the institutional church—finds itself today? We obviously cannot continue on the path we are on now. There will be no "reassertion of authority" that will be persuasive. Vatican II will not be gutted nor denied. Yet we seem to have dug ourselves such a deep hole that it seems there is no possible way to get out.

I submit that the answer lies in a proper understanding of what the Roman Catholic Church means by the word *tradition* and a recommitment by the church to the place of *reason* in determining truth.

For most people, even many educated Catholics, tradition implies "traditional," as in "this is the way we've always done it." In this sense, tradition is a conservative force that tends to prevent change from happening. Tradition is seen as a way to recreate the past. This is not, however, the proper Catholic understanding of tradition. Tradition is a way for the People of God, which is the church, to read the signs of the times and invent the future. It is a liberating force, not an inhibiting one.

The Roman Catholic Church has always felt that there were two sources of what we call "Revelation": the Bible and Tradition. This is a very radical idea. It means that Catholics do not, as many Protestant Christians do, believe in *"sola scriptura,"* or "Scripture alone," as the only way to know the will of God or the history of salvation. Instead, Catholics believe that God's revelation can also be known in the lived experience of faithful Christians over the centuries. It is tradition that gives us our devotion to Mary and the saints, that allowed us to change the Sabbath from Saturday to Sunday, that led to our support of labor unions and the preferential option for the poor, that helped us develop our metaphor of the seamless garment of life, that ultimately will show us the way on issues such as war and capital punishment.

• • • • • •

We need to allow people to observe, judge, and act—not just on issues in our world but on issues in our church.

• • • • • •

Tradition is really the basis for the very idea of the *magisterium* of the church. It says that the church, under the protection of the Holy Spirit, will not and cannot make a mistake on the really important matters of faith and morals. It also says that the church is a living organism that can learn and change by listening to the "lived experience" of the faithful.

The Catholic Church is not a fundamentalist sect. We can respond to what Vatican II called "the signs of the times" and adapt what we do and even how we believe and worship based on our experience as the People of God. I submit that tradition will be the way out of our current quandary regarding a long list of different and difficult issues. We need to embrace tradition, understand what it really means, and begin to really exercise it. We need to allow people to observe, judge, and act—not just on issues in our world but on issues in our church.

To do so, however, we must use our ability to reason.

Just a few millennia ago, Aristotle was convinced that the heavier an object the faster it would fall to the ground. And who would have disagreed with Aristotle, the greatest thinker of his time? But if the scientific methodology of experimentation and research, with its rubric of reasoning and empirical observation, were available then, the truth would have been known. All that it would have taken for him to see that he was wrong was for Aristotle to take a heavy and a light object, drop them to the ground from some height, and observe what happened. With all of his genius, why didn't Aristotle do that? Or, why didn't someone else think of it?

However, it was two millennia later, in 1589, that a Catholic layman, Galileo Galilei, gathered the *cognoscenti* of his time to the Leaning Tower of Pisa. There, from the top of the tower, he simultaneously pushed off a ten-pound and a one-pound weight. Everyone at the base of the Tower could not help but observe that both weights landed at the same exact time. Yet, history tells us that all those learned observers who witnessed this event denied what they had seen. They continued to believe that Aristotle was correct, and thought they observed that the heavier object fell to the ground first. Indeed, they were not to be confused by the facts, and the power of conventional wisdom remained intact.

It was not until the Renaissance, in particular in the sixteenth century, with its overwhelming interest in humanism and an intense curiosity in the phenomena of nature, that the empirical approach to the discovery of truth—the scientific method—gained respectability. As a result, there evolved distrust in conventional wisdom and authoritative pronouncements of any kind.

Two centuries later, in eighteenth century Europe, the *philosophie des lumieres* went even further in opposing traditional belief in authority, in traditional doctrines, and in wisdom and cultural norms. This "Enlightenment"—by the light of reason—was now the spreading and accepted paradigm for progress and the intellectual development of people. Indeed, people did not see things as they saw them in past times. So striking was this new way to see reality and facts that Immanuel Kant said this was humankind's emergence from its self-inflicted tutelage. Clearly, the facts did not change, but now people saw those same facts differently.

People began to see the things that were always there but interpreted them quite differently than they traditionally had. And once people perceive reality differently, there will inevitably follow change, transformation, and death of old paradigms. Thus, looking at history in that emerging milieu of scientific positivism, one can see the verdant pastures and abundant harvests of technological growth: the printing press, the steam engine, the radio, the airplane, television, the computer, the internet. Each has, in its own way and interconnected with other technologies, exponentially changed its contemporaneous world and, of course, all of the worlds that have followed.

What must be understood in terms of the current quandary inside the church, what history throughout the millennia has demonstrated, is that no one, no authority, and no institution can ultimately prevent or stop people from seeing the facts before them and using their rational abilities to seek the truth in the reality they perceive. This lesson seems to be the most difficult lesson for any institution to accept, and especially difficult for any organized religion. Yet in so many ways the opposite should be true, especially in the Catholic Church, which has for centuries professed belief in the complementary nature of faith and reason. This conviction has been the foundation and the central focus of the magnificence in the church's rich intellectual tradition.

Recently, however, faithful Catholics are having difficulty seeing this quality in the *modus operandi* and institutional culture of the church. And, it is not only the manner in which the church irrationally and inappropriately handled the many horrendous sexual abuse cases that have singularly caused this negative perception. A practicing Catholic woman recently anecdotally captured in a letter to the editor what many faithful are seeing in the actions of the institutional church. Of course, she had to send the letter to a secular press in order to vent her frustration and dismay. On August 24, 2010, a newspaper in the upper Midwest region of the U.S. printed her letter:

> I grew up Catholic. I've always felt I've known what it means to be Catholic. Lately I question whether I do know what it means to be Catholic due to events I have witnessed in my parish. Does being Catholic mean I have no voice in my parish? Concerns expressed to my pastor and the diocese have gone unheeded. Does being Catho-

lic mean accepting that family members are not welcomed to attend Mass with me, even though they believe in the same God? Does being Catholic mean I need to sit by passively while the future of my child's spiritual education is in doubt and no one will answer the questions I have? Does being Catholic mean I must obediently shut my eyes, ears, and lips to the pain of others because the church says I must not question the authority of a hierarchy that won't listen to the concerns of its people? Everything I was taught growing up must be false. To me, being Catholic means something entirely different from what I am being told. Being Catholic should mean speaking out against injustice, embracing all who believe in God, taking an active role in the faith of my child, and shining the light of Christ where there is darkness.

In essence, with an intellectual commitment to faith being complementary to reason, the institutional church should encourage open and widely inclusive dialogue among all. It should trust in reason and common sense applied to the church, just as it should be to everything else. With all its good intentions, the institutional church falls into the terrible traps of paternalism and authoritarianism while trying to protect the faithful from competing values and possible heresy. Yet, even assuming such good intentions, this—once again—is the fact of reality: No one, no authority, and no institution can prevent people from using their rational abilities to seek the truth. And, more importantly, no authority—even the institutional church's hierarchy—should be able to prevent people from exercising their conscience, their personal and communal relationship with God, and their own power of reason. The Holy Spirit is alive and well in the church. After all, it is the Holy Spirit's job to "fill the hearts of the faithful and kindle in them the fire of God's love."

But it is only through a new commitment to tradition and reason as a source of wisdom that the Holy Spirit will begin to unravel the quandary that the church finds itself in today.

CHAPTER 5

The Spiritual Geography of Globalization

· · · · · ·

*People have accused me of being in favor of globalization.
This is equivalent to accusing me
of being in favor of the sun rising in the morning.*

CLARE SHORT

· · · · · ·

Whether one is in the halls of academia, or a cocktail lounge with some friends, or especially if one is sitting in a boardroom of a business enterprise or listening to a government or political debate, the term *globalization* will inevitably be heard loudly, clearly, and often *ad nauseum*. The only place you don't hear it that much is in the institutional church. Of course, the Catholic Church has always prided itself in its global reach, but that is a far cry from understanding what globalization means in the contemporary world. It has changed everything.

Globalization has become a term that is most easily understood in the world of business. It describes a process that has integrated the world of finance into a worldwide, complicated network that has never before been realized on Earth. Though its economic beginnings develop right after World War II with the decisions coming from the Bretton Woods Conference, it has been in the last two decades that it took hold in the world "writ large."

The Bretton Woods Conference is a name commonly given to the United Nations Monetary and Financial Conference, held in the summer of 1944, at Bretton Woods, New Hampshire. The conference resulted in the creation of the

International Monetary Fund to promote international monetary cooperation, and the beginning of—or creation of—the International Bank for Reconstruction and Development. By December 1945 the required number of governments had ratified the treaties creating the two organizations and by the summer of 1946 they had begun operation.

That Conference quite successfully broke down the national walls that obstructed an open and free flow of activities in international commerce. Thus, even if we attempt to explain the global financial intricacies and infrastructure of this economic globalization process, the likely reality is that none of us fully grasps its ongoing effects. In fact, though, the end results are not difficult to understand: With all its problems, deficiencies, and sometimes unethical and corrupt practices, economic globalization is a meaningful yet worrisome reality. It is a fact of third millennium life and continues to hold significant promise in efforts to reduce global poverty.

• • • • • •

Information and knowledge have become democratized and are no longer in the sole domain of governments, the powerful, and those in authority.

• • • • • •

However, globalization is even more difficult to grasp when we consider that even economic globalization, with all its complexity, is simpler to understand than the more expansive reality of comprehensive globalization as a total process. In the totality of globalization, nations, societies, cultures, and religions are immediately and permanently affected by the emerging advances in a globally interconnected network of communications, technology, transportation, and economics.

Because of globalization, information and knowledge have become democratized and are no longer in the sole domain of governments, the powerful, and those in authority from everything from the Boy Scouts of America to, well, the Roman Catholic Church. In a globalized world people want to know everything that is knowable and expect to be able to learn it at "wikispeed." In a globalized world people will know everything that they want to know, even if they have to write it themselves! Never before in history has there been such immediacy and connectivity possible among people about their ideas, values, world-views, and religious beliefs. The world is indeed shrinking, but concurrently its problems are growing.

In a globalized world, clashing cultural, religious, and ideological dynamics permeate societal reasoning with diverse forces. For example, it is clear that one group's "freedom fighters" are another group's "terrorists." Or one group's "orthodoxy" is another group's "heresy." The new generations are growing up in a world that is no longer round but flat, as Thomas Friedman recently told us in his 2005 bestseller, *The World is Flat*. By this image Friedman tried to capture the reality and implications of the "shrinking globe" and the ubiquitous information and opinion available to everyone from the most to the least privileged.

In another image, expounded by Frances Cairncross, known for her work in *The Economist*, she notes that not only is the world now flat but "distance" is also dead—thus the title of her book, *The Death of Distance*. The young on this globe have grown up with a new "transport system" brought about by the electronic and technological innovations in communications and travel. They no longer see the world as foreign or exotic or unknowable. This globalized society not only has new quantitative effects but also awesome qualitative implications. If the church does not understand, respect, and respond to this, it will no longer be able to effectively spread the Good News.

There is much technology now available to the church that is not simply new but also of remarkably fine quality. But this technology also plays a dominant role in the dramatic, existential change in human behavior and perceptions that have transformed how people today see everything, including religion.

Most of us who are more advanced in our chronological measurement (that is, we "old folks") grew up in a spherical and physical geography within a quantifiable and definable space. But the world's new generations are growing up in a new, intangible, interactive, interconnected, interweaving, instantaneous, and technological reality that is best described as a "spiritual geography." Not a "religious geography," but a spiritual geography.

This new, global spiritual geography exists more within cyberspace than in those geographical "ports" found on maps, such as our beautiful church and school buildings, more in inquisitive minds, imaginations, and sensibilities than in doctrinal truths found in official church documents.

The burden falls upon the church in this globalized society, on this shrinking—quite shrunk already—planet to develop a more effective and universal message that can be embraced by the growing, multifarious, incommensurable, and diverse variety of people on this newly globalized planet.

It is certainly incumbent upon the church to speak the truth as it sees it, but we must speak it in a way that can be understood within the evolving spiritual geography of the third millennium. It should be emphasized that the essence of evangelization in a globalized society is not necessarily bringing people to the church but rather bringing Christ to the people.

It seems that the generations of those growing up in the spiritual geography of cyberspace do not rely on the more rational and dogmatic sphere of knowing, which is intrinsically familiar to older generations of us faithful. It is certainly not that the new generations are less rational or cerebral; rather, they form their ideas and beliefs in a world that is no longer primarily spatial or objective. The spiritual geography of the new generations challenges them with a distance-free, wide-open, and unrestricted globalized world reality.

Many of us, of whatever age, have discovered that it is on the shrinking globe (this flat and, in many ways, distance-free world) that we are brought together "cyber-physically," almost in a geo-physical togetherness. Unfortunately, at the same time, this globalization separates the older and the newer generations more profoundly than they have ever been before in the history of civilization. The church must begin to embrace this new reality and understand it as a qualitatively, profoundly different way of seeing and doing things.

The institutional church, throughout its history, has always been an international force. Within its pervasive and keenly managed worldwide diplomatic infrastructure, the institutional church has its listening posts almost everywhere on the globe. And when it does not have the legal sanction to be in a particular geographic area officially, the church has been quite successful in its unique ability to somehow have an unofficial yet effective underground presence where it is not desired. (Just ask the Chinese about this institutional church phenomenon.) So, for the institutional church internationalization is not something new. In fact, the Roman Catholic Church is an expert at it. However, the problem is that *internationalization* is simply not the same as *globalization*. The new dynamic of the globalized world is quite different from the previous paradigm in which internationalization involved the ability to listen and see others and their different ways in different parts of the world, but having done our listening and observing the aim of the "internationalized" church was to foster its own worldview and thrust its own cultural terms upon those others who were different. That is simply not going to happen anymore.

The institutional church in the past, of course, taught all nations its own culturally conditioned version of the Good News. Its "missionary" paradigm focused on indigenous people being indoctrinated to the philosophical and theological constructs that were aimed at and understandable to a person of Western sensibilities and culture. These constructs were not necessarily relevant to non-Western people, but it just didn't matter what they "thought." The institutional church had the truth and others simply needed to change their thinking and get on board! On our shrinking globe now, however, the connectivity with and integration of other worldviews are no longer just a matter of the church recognizing the curious and novel ways others "misunderstand" reality.

> *But how can globalization not change also how and where people now journey on their religious or spiritual journeys?*

The new reality system brought about by the electronic and technological revolution is not only seen in communications and travel but also in the spoken and unspoken languages of diverse people; in their psychological and aesthetic sensitivities; and in their relationships with authority, schools, and, yes, even the church. Globalization certainly changed economies, politics, travel, and communications; that is clear. So how can globalization not change how and where people now journey on their religious or spiritual journeys?

The church's mission is, of course, still alive. We are to proclaim that the kingdom of God has begun in the person of Jesus Christ. However, over the centuries, that mission fostered a faith that existed in a spherical and physical world within quantifiable and definable space and time. That now-dying

Catholic world was mired in predictability, continuity, certainty, and control. Understandably, that world is much more attractive to today's institutional church. However, the ever-growing numbers of those conditioned to live in a world that is now "flat" experience a much different reality on the globalized journey they are now taking.

The institutional church is no longer presenting its important and vital Good News to a docile and receptive audience that is passively waiting to be told what to think and do. Now those embedded in the globalized world (and the "embedding" is beginning even in pre-teen years) are producing their own "You Tube" media presentations or incessantly and compulsively sending ever-so-brief messages via their "Twittering" capabilities or creatively composing their own *personae* on "Facebook" and countless blogs. This momentum is not going to be stopped. Globalization can only be a clarion death knell for any institution that ignores it and thinks it is only a passing fad.

It is not easy for any institution to make an overwhelmingly drastic change in how it views itself. How much more difficult is it for any religious group to accept this? How much more difficult, then, for the Catholic Church—which has such a rich and significant history of accomplishing its mission—to respond to a new way of doing the things that it holds sacred? Historically, the church has had difficulty when drastic cultural change takes place that requires a different mode of operation. Instead of seeing the new advance as an opportunity to make its mission more effective in a world that has *de facto* changed how it communicates, the institution fears that its very existence is under attack.

It is, of course, difficult for the institutional church to adapt to this newly globalized world because so many of the leaders within the institutional church today interpret what they see as an attack upon the universal and unchanging truth of its sacred depository of faith. But it must change how it proclaims that Good News. Otherwise, it will become irrelevant as it continues to confuse its timeless message with how it proclaims that truth in a globalized world.

CHAPTER 6

Communion and Democratization

• • • • • •

I hope to have communion with the people,
that is the most important thing.

Pope John Paul II

• • • • • •

A colleague described an incident in which he took a taxi from the Vatican, where he had just finished attending a meeting, to the De LaSalle Brothers' residence where I now live in Rome. The Italian taxi driver struck up a conversation with him about the church and the recent financial and sex abuse scandals. My colleague became curious as to the "faithfulness" of this man who identified himself as a Catholic.

He asked the driver, "Do you consider yourself a practicing Catholic?"

The driver answered with conviction, "Yes, I am."

Then he asked the driver, "Well, do you go to Mass every Sunday?"

The driver abruptly twisted his head to the back of the taxi and curtly answered, "I said I was a Catholic, not a fanatic!"

If this were really a joke, we could all have a good laugh and go on with church business as usual. But it is not a joke, and it reveals what many in the institutional church would not care to admit about how most (and by that I mean at least a majority of) Catholics see ourselves today in relationship to the church. Gone are the days when we would consider ourselves Catholic to the degree that we routinely followed all the prescribed rubrics of church practices, rules, and obligations. Gone, too, are the days when most of us cared about how we are perceived by the institutional church. (If you don't believe me on this, just go to Mass on any given Sunday and look around. Or just look at the number of children that most Catholic families now have and tell me that most of them are not practicing some form of "artificial" birth control.)

It would be an unjust assessment for anyone to judge that we who are not in lock-step with all the outward signs of behavior that the church prescribes are therefore "less Catholic" than we used to be or the institutional church wants us to be. In fact, the reaction of institutional church leaders is to try to close the barn door after the horse has already gone. They think if they "reassert" their authority and insist on everyone following all outward manifestations of their personal religious beliefs and practices they will restore the church they once knew. It ain't gonna happen!

We may better understand the heart of this quandary in the divided church of today's globalized world by grasping the historical development of ecclesiology as it pertains to *"koinonia,* or *"communio."* *Koinonia* is the Greek and *communio* is the Latin word frequently used in the New Testament to describe the intimate and collegial fellowship desired within the church; in English the word is *communion.*

This chapter utilizes the fine study of theologian Judith K. Schaefer, OP. In her book *The Evolution of a Vow: Obedience as Decision Making in Communion,* she presents a theological investigation of the vow of obedience in relation to the exercise of authority in the church. Although Schaefer is particularly addressing an understanding of obedience with an emphasis on women and men religious in the church, nevertheless she unfolds a cogent exposition of communion and what it can mean in a wider context for the church. (How I synthesize, extrapolate, and select themes from Schaefer are my responsibility and in no way should reflect on her intentions or her amazing objectivity. So, hopefully the bishops won't call her on the carpet because of me.)

At the heart of much tension in the church today are these two complexly interrelated questions:

- Just what does it mean to be a good, practicing—not to be interpreted as fanatical—Catholic?
- And to what degree must we be explicitly "obedient" to all pronouncements and directives of the church's hierarchy?

Controversy abounds over dictums promulgated by the institutional church and its insistence that to be a practicing Catholic one must fully accept all the articulations of the hierarchy-defined doctrine and morality. In some cases the hierarchy even asserts that there may be no further discussion on something that does not fall even remotely into the realm of doctrine or morality, e.g., women's ordination. Topics that "good" Catholics are not expected to discuss include issues such as birth control, homosexual unions, spiritual pluralism, and the role of women in the church's priestly ministry. The list, of course, goes on and on.

And to what degree must we be explicitly "obedient" to all pronouncements and directives of the church's hierarchy?

For example, extreme controversy has been precipitated by official institutional church pronouncements that insist that even in Africa, where AIDS is a pandemic that often infects completely innocent married women, condom use is sinful. In such circumstances, we are told by the hierarchy that the women should simply practice abstinence. However, many (including some African bishops) have tried to explain to their colleagues that most of the time infected husbands insist or, worse yet, force their wives to have sex with them even when the men know that they already have AIDS. Millions of innocent African women have already died, and many millions more will die, if condoms are not used. So, is it any wonder that many of them say, "Obviously, these old, unmarried men in Rome care more about their abstract rules than our very lives. Don't they realize that that is the opposite of what Jesus taught us?"

Some consider this to be a rude and unfair thing to say about men who are trying to profess what they believe to be true. Nevertheless, common sense, in alliance with the Christian spirit, compels such institutional church pronouncements to be open for discussion by any faithful follower of Christ. This is the very nature of tradition, properly understood, in the church. To stop discussion on an issue related to such a devastating catastrophe could never be the correct or Christian thing to do. It also certainly gives rise to allegations of hypocrisy in a church that has recently been riddled with sexual abuse cases and cover-ups. How can any sensitive and thinking person be surprised at such controversial reactions of many of the faithful to these kinds of things? Perhaps a better understanding of the role of communion in the context of such controversies in the church can be helpful.

"Communion ecclesiology," which emphasizes a radical change from earlier understandings about holiness, became evident at the Second Vatican Council. All in the church were exhorted to renew the church's role in the modern world. The church was no longer to see itself as separate from the world or its problems:

> Nothing that is genuinely human fails to find an echo in (the followers of Christ's) hearts.... That is why they cherish a feeling of deep solidarity with the human race and its history (*Gaudium et Spes* 1).

This new communion ecclesiology emphasizes the universal call to holiness for all of us, not just those in the institutional church. In essence, this goal of holiness of all in the church *de facto* democratizes dialogue in the church. A church built on communion necessitates the participation of all of us, in all our diversity. Yet to this day many of the institutional church leaders resist this kind of democratization and hold on to the older, much more authoritarian image of the church. Instead of "communion," they have brought back "ex-communion" as their strategy of choice.

This presents another quandary for the institutional church today that is in need of unraveling. These are the two competing models at hand for "being" and "doing" church.

Contributing to these opposing approaches was *Lumen Gentium's* introduction of a new image of the church that included not only the clergy and religious but also the laity as participants in the mission of Christ as Prophet, Priest, and King. All were reminded—even the laity—that we all participate in the saving mission of the church. This, then, is the blossoming of the concept of the church as the People of God. With this new understanding, how can anyone—especially the members of the hierarchy who insist that everyone else acquiesce to them—not accept what emerged from Vatican II, which was a radical change in the church's identity. And it must necessarily follow that with this model of church the organizational functioning of the church must change.

• • • • • •

Vatican II truly awakened all the faithful to the active presence of the Holy Spirit and the Spirit's gifts that are given to all the faithful—not just to those leading the institutional church.

• • • • • •

Yet we see subtle, carefully nuanced, and steady movement within the institutional church of late to reject this new open and democratized model and return to an older, more rigid, hierarchical model of church. In this instance, it may be justifiable for some of us to turn the tables and criticize some of the incorrectly called "traditionalists" as being the "cafeteria Catholics." Aren't they the ones who are picking and choosing what to accept as authentic Catholicism?

In the Vatican II model of church, then, communion ought to conjure descriptors of the church in terms such as collegiality, subsidiarity, collaboration, participative decision-making, dialogue, sharing of power, gender equality, and acceptance of diversity (including sexual orientation). However, when we begin to introduce such democratizing descriptors of church it implies a reliance on and a faith in an expanded role for the Holy Spirit. As Vatican II reminded us:

When the work which the Father gave to the Son to do on earth was completed, the Holy Spirit was sent on the day of Pentecost to sanctify the church continually (*Lumen Gentium* 4).

Indeed, Vatican II truly awakened all the faithful to the active presence of the Holy Spirit and the Spirit's gifts that are given to all the faithful—not just to those leading the institutional church.

Currently, the two competing models of "being" and "doing" church are generating the divisive split in the church, and it revolves around "communion," both in general and specifically regarding the reception of the consecrated bread and wine. On the one side, there is a focus on *unity* that is manifested in hierarchical authority and quite obviously conforms to centralized decision-making. The recent efforts of a few bishops in the United States to regulate and withhold the cup from most Catholics most of the time is an example of this effort at control that has run amok.

The late Holy Father, John Paul II, and the current Pope, Benedict XVI, have opposed any kind of intercommunion with other Christian churches. On the other side, theologians such as J.M.R. Tillard and Cardinal Walter Kasper have presented a meaningful opposing view in their writing on communion in the church. For them, unity encompasses and includes diversity within the broader church. They believe the joint reception of communion can further ecumenical dialogue.

Of course, our various viewpoints on the issue of communion will lead to different approaches to the attainment of unity, or even how to define unity. Without some agreement on which of the models of church can be embraced by the faithful, the very nature of the future church will be immersed in controversy. It would seem to me, however, that a model of church that emphasizes inclusivity—since it fosters unity more in line with Vatican II's focus on church as community and seeks participation of the faithful through the power of the Holy Spirit—should be the one we seek going forward. Significantly present in this ecclesiological model are the dynamics of subsidiarity, collaboration, shared responsibility, and acceptance of diversity. These attributes are difficult to see in today's institutional church and the hierarchy's recent behavior in dealing with their mistakes and controversies.

When we take into consideration the scriptural basis for the ideal of communion in the church, it is difficult to accept the more rigid and authoritarian model that many in the hierarchy seem to embrace. Many of the institutional church leaders of late espouse collegiality, but they certainly do not act as if they are open to questioning by the faithful with differing views. They resort to demanding internal assent, not permitting certain topics to even be discussed, using ex-communication as a control discipline, and controlling access to the Body and Blood of Christ. These are not indications of a biblical spirit of *koinonia* or *communio*.

Koinonia, as it unfolds in a communion ecclesiology, uses the image of the Holy Trinity to help us understand the nature of the church. It emphasizes that our Triune God as three divine Persons who are distinct from each other. It reflects a diversity of images for us to see. At the same time, the three persons are united and are one God in three divine persons. This image of communion is poignantly described by theologian Judith Schaefer as:

> ...an analogous way to image the divine Godhead; it describes the relationships among the triune Persons as equal yet distinct, and as unified while being diverse. Communion ecclesiology is intrinsically about relationships of unity that include and require elements of diversity.

With the foundational theology of church presented with this image of *koinonia*, the institutional church should be compelled to be authentic in the way it exercises its true authority, with great attention to the challenge to bring unity out of diversity. This can happen only if the constitutive element and dynamic of an effective collegiality is operating and effectively present through actions and practices. Or again, as Schaeffer expressed it:

> Freely communicating with one another, both speaking and listening, the persons of the Trinity exhibit a coexistence of unity within plurality. Their *koinonia*, or communion, is what constitutes the church intrinsically; all else—structure, organization, and membership—flows from communion.

It is this type of unity that the faithful and the world need if the church is to bring people, all people, together in the caring and sharing spirit that Jesus has called us to be. In a globalized society, church unity must co-exist with diversity. Without this communion, fragmentation, ideological in-fighting, and mean-spiritedness will continue to exist in the church and prevent us from carrying out our mission to proclaim the reign of God "on earth as it is in heaven." The institutional church must support and foster a collegiality with all the faithful that makes *communio* real and effective. It must see that this type of communion in the church (and intercommunion with our non-Catholic brethren) does not diminish the Catholic Church's authority, but rather enhances it and makes it fair and just and much more responsive to Jesus' call that we may all be one.

• • • • • •

Without this communion mean-spiritedness will continue to exist in the church and prevent us from carrying out our mission to proclaim the reign of God "on earth as it is in heaven."

• • • • • •

Let us not be naïve. The church as *koinonia* is a model that encourages collaboration and subsidiarity, although it produces a "messy" church. Such a model fosters a spirit of openness and dialogue that is less susceptible to control and contains no guarantee of how it will work. This type of existence will not be comfortable for the current institutional church's methodology. Therefore, this is a major quandary for the church, because many in its power structure view such democratization as a threat to their focus on the church as absolute hierarchical authority and centralized decision-maker. It is well to remind those adherents of a rigid control structure, who like to say that the church is not a democracy, of the words of a pope they often quote, John Paul II, in his encyclical *Redemptor Hominis*:

> The Church wishes to serve this single end: that each person may be able to find Christ, in order that Christ may walk with each person the path of life…. The Church is the community of disciples, each of whom in a different way—at times very consciously and consistently, at other times, not very consciously and very consistently—is following Christ. This shows also the deeply "personal" aspect and dimension of this society.

CHAPTER 7

The Nobility of Difference

• • • • • •

I take as my guide the hope of a saint:
in crucial things, unity;
in important things, diversity;
in all things, generosity.

GEORGE H. W. BUSH

• • • • • •

Some Catholics earnestly fear that a more open church that welcomes diversity and pluralism will lead people to accept competing values or beliefs as equal to the Gospel. This attitude was poignantly and strikingly addressed at a presentation given by then Cardinal Joseph Ratzinger immediately before the College of Cardinals went into the conclave that elected him pope. Ratzinger warned the cardinals of the current global culture that is promoting what he called a "dictatorship of relativism." Ratzinger came out of that conclave as Pope Benedict XVI, so we know that the issue is on the minds of the leaders of the institutional church. Let us now investigate the quandary the church finds itself in regarding the highly charged issue of relativism, and see how tradition, properly understood, might help unravel it.

In the early 1950s, then-famous movie actor George Raft was asked at a press conference, "Mr. Raft you have made millions of dollars in your career, and it is now reported that you have lost almost all that money. What happened?" Raft paused, collected his thoughts, and nonchalantly responded, "Well, you see, over these past years I spent a great deal of money gambling on the horses, a lot on boozing it up, and a huge amount on womanizing. The rest of the money I spent foolishly."

We could all have an extended conversation on whether Mr. Raft's diverse proclivities to relax and enjoy his own hard-earned money were, shall we say, justifiable. Many of us might conclude that his priorities and values leave much to be desired and certainly reflect on his deficient personal values. But his humorous response might also lead us to reflect on just how far we can go in our assessment of the actions and judgments of other individuals and institutions in this multicultural, shrinking world of ours.

We must be able to dialogue with others about these issues without self-righteousness, embarrassment, or fear

As I mentioned earlier, this shrinking world of ours has produced sharply different and competing ways of looking at the world. These differences in values and beliefs have also resulted in an abundance of hatred and terrorism. Most caring, honest people of good will do not hesitate to accept that in today's globalized society there must be respect and sensitivity for diverse religions, belief systems, and societal mores. However, we are quick to add that a line must be drawn and we cannot accept all values and beliefs as equal and acceptable. There is only one "slight," double-faceted problem with this: Where is the line to be drawn; and who does the drawing?

It does seem reasonable for us to be on guard lest we fall into the trap of ancient fourth-century BCE Greek philosophers, the "Sophists." They taught that all human judgment is subjective and that ultimate reality involves only one's own perspective. (Perhaps, George Raft was a Sophist.) A dilemma arises, however, as to whether or when a personal or religiously held belief can be justifiably imposed on someone who believes differently. This is especially troublesome for the church that believes it has the "fullness of truth" because it is the church of Jesus Christ, the Son of God, the savior of the world.

Where does the church draw the line? How the church can accept a plurality of views and a diversity of lifestyles and yet not permit itself to fall into the

Sophist trap is the quandary that needs unraveling here. First, we must learn to accept and celebrate differences among people of good will. Second, we must be able to seek difficult but reasonable compromises rather than try (certainly unsuccessfully) to impose rigid, dogmatic dictums on people who don't agree with us. Third, we must be able to dialogue with others about these issues without self-righteousness, embarrassment, or fear.

Complicating the work for the institutional church in this regard is another quandary. There was a myth when globalization began that there would naturally follow a process of homogenization of world cultures and even religions. While there is some truth that popular culture, from music to movies, has become more homogenous, what has also emerged is a worldwide movement toward greater diversity, with an emphasis on uniqueness and individuality. This is true even in religion.

How do we act in this kind of world with a plurality of viewpoints without resorting to relativism? How does the institutional church react to diversity so that, by its actions, it can help teach us to be caring, sensitive, and respectful proclaimers of the Gospel without losing our own moral and religious compass?

It is first important to grasp the distinctions of the terms *diversity*, *pluralism*, and *relativism*, since they are not really interchangeable in their meanings. A book could be written on each of these words if one is trying to present a thorough exposition. There are myriad political, cultural, philosophical, biological, religious nuances for each of them. For our purposes, however, let us utilize a simple, straightforward, and general approach to differentiating these concepts.

The least difficult of these notions to approach intellectually and practically is *diversity*. Because it is the most benign of the three concepts, it is very widely accepted by most people. Diversity is simply the recognition of a quality or practice that expresses a state of being different from other qualities or practices. Most people who are not closed-minded can and do accept diversity in this world of growing interconnectedness. Many, though not all, world religions accept for instance the right of other religions to practice and promote their different beliefs. We call this "freedom of religion," and it is one of the main contributions of the United States of America's experiment in democracy, although some people are always trying to subvert it and establish Christianity as the "official" religion of the U.S.A.

Pluralism introduces a bit more complex situation, especially with groups of competing religions. While a particular religion may acknowledge diversity by recognizing the freedom of anyone to practice a particular religion, this does not extend necessarily to an acceptance of the precepts of the other religion. Pluralism involves at least the tolerance of those other views, values, and beliefs. To acknowledge pluralism, then, is to accept that your creed may not necessarily be the sole one that is true and right for all. That stance is a rather more difficult for most religions to embrace. It has certainly been a problem historically for the Roman Catholic Church, from the Crusades through the Inquisition even to today.

Finally and most problematic for most organized religions—especially for the institutional church—is the strong and developing world movement toward *relativism*. Relativism goes beyond pluralism in that it not only recognizes and accepts the right to hold other views but also makes no judgments as to the rightness or wrongness of opposing views. In other words, for the relativist, there are no universal truths. For them, we must all judge the validity of values and morals based on the circumstances and belief systems of those who espouse them or who act upon them. Some characterize relativism in a pejorative manner by saying that it is a doctrine which stands for "Anything Goes!" Maybe George Raft was a relativist.

How can the institutional church unravel this serious quandary precipitated by the strong international dynamics favoring universal acceptance of relativistic forces or, as Pope Benedict XVI described it, the "dictatorship of relativism?" This kind of ambiguity is not something that has just landed on the doorstep of the institutional church. We see, even in Vatican II, concern about diversity and how it can bring about unity in the church without causing division:

A diversity of members and functions is engaged in the building up of Christ's body, too. There is only one Spirit who, out of his own richness and the needs of the ministries, gives his various gifts for the welfare of the church.... The same Spirit who of himself is the principle of unity in the body, by his own power and by the interior cohesion of the members, produces and stimulates love among the faithful (*Lumen Gentium* 7).

If the church does not act in an efficacious manner in a world filled with diversity and pluralism on a shrinking globe, then we are doomed to irrelevance at best. However, if we avoid a "dictatorship of relativism" and replace it with a "dictatorship of authoritarianism," which employs rigid control of peoples' freedom, prevents them from thinking for themselves, and restricts open dialogue with others not like ourselves, then destructive clashes will inevitably ensue, both among those inside and with those outside the church. All should heed the insightful comment of theologian J.M.R. Tillard in his book *Flesh of the Church*:

> Indeed, difference is intrinsic to the communion which constitutes the church; difference is one of the components of this communion. The church is neither abolition nor addition, but communion of differences.... By causing the common reality hidden under differences to emerge, one manifests a communion, one reveals the riches of unity, one acknowledges the nobility of difference.

The nobility of difference! What a powerful and magnificent image. It is an epiphany of sorts that is sorely needed in our troubled global society. Rabbi Jonathan Sacks provides some impressive insights on these very points in his book *The Dignity of Difference: How to Avoid the Clash of Civilizations*. Rabbi Sacks, although a conservative rabbinic scholar, has some very pragmatic advice regarding acceptance of pluralism by religions. So pragmatic were his insights that many "ultra-orthodox" rabbis accused Sacks of heresy. They consider his caring, sensitive, and loving outreach to other religions as an endorsement of "Relativism," because he does not place Jewish religious teaching ahead of peoples' life situations. (Hmmm. Doesn't that sound familiar to us Catholics?)

Sacks utilizes a parable of a Jewish mystic leader who attempts to bring out the essence of a religion that embraces exclusivity in its teaching and spirituality to the exclusion of the beauty and values to be gained from other religions.

> Imagine, he said, two people who spend their lives transporting stones. One carries bags of diamonds. The other hauls sacks of rocks. Each is now asked to take a consignment of rubies. Which of the two understands what he is now to carry? The man who is used to diamonds knows that stones can be precious, even those that are not diamonds. But the man who has carried only rocks thinks of stones as a mere burden. They have weight but not worth. Rubies are beyond his comprehension.

The moral of Sacks' story is that if we cherish our own faith we will understand the value of others' faith. He further elaborates that though we regard our faith as diamonds and that of others as rubies, we at least recognize that both are precious stones.

How far should we Catholics go in demonstrating our dedication and commitment to bring about respect in this world by having the courage to embrace the "other"? The answer: until we make real our love for the different and understand it is God who created the dignity of difference itself.

• • • • • •

If we cherish our own faith we will understand the value of others' faith.

• • • • • •

Similar thoughts were expressed in May, 2010, by Cardinal Marc Ouellet, then of Quebec City (now the Prefect of the Congregation for Bishops), at the Catholic Media Convention in Toronto. He pointed out that, "Evangelization also involves a sincere dialogue that seeks to understand the reasons and feelings of others." Ouellet clearly told his audience, "To evangelize does not mean simply to teach a doctrine but to proclaim Jesus Christ by one's words and actions...." He exhorted those gathered to action with the thought: "New evangelization means to dare once again, and with the humility of the small grain, to leave up to God the when and how it will grow."

The quandary in the institutional church today involves the many faithful who enthusiastically endorse the beautifully espoused thoughts of Cardinal Oullet yet see the actual *modus operandi* of many in the hierarchy who act in a rigid, uncompromising, authoritative, and dogmatic manner. It does not appear to many of us that they are disposed toward acting in a way that would clearly demonstrate the need for the "dialogue," "understanding," and "humility" of which Cardinal Oullet speaks. Instead of the institutional church trying to deny this situation, it should seek ways to be more open to changing structures in order to better manifest its commitment to the nobility of difference.

There are far more reasons for us Catholics to be worried about our "turning off" our dialogue with the world and with other religions than in our "turning into" relativists. Until all religions, nations, and cultures can go beyond a mere tolerance for a world already immersed in pluralism and learn to appreciate the overwhelming contribution that diversity brings to the world, we will not have peace. And how much more should the Catholic Church, with its core Gospel value of love for all, even our enemies, be a light of the world, demonstrating that it is possible to overcome differences without being worried about diminishing the truth of our Christian message? Understanding and appreciating another's viewpoint does not weaken our commitment to our own beliefs. It does not make us relativists. It makes us good Christians.

CHAPTER 8

Women's Ordination: An Exercise in Tradition

· · · · · ·

*Catholic men are more upset
about women not being able to be priests
than are Catholic women.*

FATHER ANDREW GREELEY

· · · · · ·

In light of our discussion of the role of tradition, properly understood, as a way of unraveling the quandary in which the institutional church now finds itself, the next two chapters discuss a topic that is quite controversial. Consider this discussion to be in the spirit of Cardinal Marc Oullet, the Prefect for the Congregation of Bishops, who recently called for "...a sincere dialogue that seeks to understand the reasons and feelings of others." I know that various members of the hierarchy have said that I am not even allowed to write this, but let us consider this to be a "case study" in how tradition is supposed to work: Over time, the Holy Spirit fills the hearts of the faithful; we speak; revelation occurs.

I am a member of the faithful. I am a professed brother and member of a religious order founded by Saint John Baptist de LaSalle, the patron saint of Christian teachers, called the Institute of the Brothers of the Christian Schools or the De LaSalle Brothers. Dozens of our brothers have been canonized or beatified. We have been around for more than 300 years of the church's history—not forever, but we weren't "born yesterday" either. Technically, like all women religious and professed brothers, I am a lay person. I am certainly one of "the faithful."

Here is what I have come to believe from my 70 years of "lived experience" of the Catholic faith:

- After more than two thousand years of the Holy Spirit's living and active presence in the lives of us faithful Christians in the Catholic Church; and
- After hundreds upon hundreds of years of our being taught by the church that the one true God, the Holy Trinity, is three Divine Persons who are spirits and therefore neither male nor female; and
- After centuries of the Holy Spirit's revelation to us that all people—not just men—are made in the image and likeness of God, who is neither male nor female (or, if you prefer, both male and female); and
- After modern-day scientific and psychological evidence demonstrating to us that the obvious physical differentiation between "male and female" gives rise to the concurrent complementarity of the gender identity of "man and woman" as the occasion that brings about our unity, dignity, and equality as "persons;" and
- After the Christian faith has informed us all our lives that since Jesus Christ was both truly God and truly human, and therefore came into the world physically as a "male" but also as a "person;" and
- After a big dose of common "Christian" sense based on our lived experience that women are and should be equal to men in every way and have gifts to offer the Catholic Church that the church sorely needs; and
- After listening to the arguments put forth by the institutional church that Jesus Christ would demand anything other than the full, complete, and total equality of all "persons"—men and women—in his church and finding those arguments completely unpersuasive and often silly; and

- After observing the experience of some of our Protestant brethren and many women in the Catholic Church who feel sure that they have been called to ordination to the deaconate or priesthood, therefore
- We the faithful believe that the ordination of women not only should take place in the Catholic Church but must take place soon.

Really I have nothing further to say about this topic. This is merely a piece of "tradition in motion": the faithful telling it like it is. Reluctantly, however, circumstances compel me to say more on this topic in the next chapter.

CHAPTER 9

Unfortunately, More Has to Be Said

• • • • • •

I will feel equality has arrived
when we can elect to office women
who are as incompetent
as some of the men who are already there.

MAUREEN REAGAN

• • • • • •

Today, many believe that the Catholic Church should ordain women because in many of the "developed" areas of the world, including the United States, there is an obvious and significant shortage of priests to "man" the churches. Dioceses are being forced to close parishes and cluster several parishes together with only one priest "manning" those churches. Consequently, the frequency in providing Mass and the sacraments to the faithful must be severely limited, because the institutional church cannot stretch one "man," who is the priest, to serve all those needing the sacraments. Therefore, as the argument goes, the church should ordain women to the priesthood to solve this "manning" problem.

This position is distasteful to me, and I do not think we should accept such a line of reasoning. It says that it was fine not to ordain women when they were not needed in the parishes, but now they should be ordained since they can be "useful." (By the way, this is also used as an argument to ordain married men, which at least has the institutional church's okay in certain circumstances already, such as a Protestant minister with family joining the Catholic Church.

However, it has the distinct negative of being one more insult to women: "We would rather ordain married men, with all the problems we know that has caused historically, than consider ordaining a woman who is ready and able to take the vow of celibacy.")

To me the shortage of priests is not a reason for women's ordination. It may, however, be an embarrassing excuse to do so.

Today, many laypeople believe the Catholic Church should ordain women because the complement of a women's viewpoint might have resulted in better handling the recent sexual abuse and cover-up scandals that have come to light. This position is also distasteful to me, and I don't think we should accept such a line of reasoning either. It assumes that women—who are, indeed, equal to men in every way, including sin—could not also have had the propensity to be just as swayed as men to cover up such abuse. Women in a power structure within a closed, authoritarian institution such as the Catholic Church are just as likely to mishandle such situations as men in order to "protect" the image of the institution that provides them with their base of power. Corruption is an "equal opportunity" employer. Now, having said all that, do I believe women in power in the church might have helped prevent the cover-up? Yes, I do. In fact, some women have "blown the whistle" recently on several priests who were abusing children or stealing from the church, but usually they were ignored or, worse, blamed for being the bearers of bad news.

• • • • • •

How can the institutional church now change that tradition without admitting that they have been wrong all these years?

• • • • • •

But still, in my opinion this is not a good reason for ordaining women. It may, however, be an embarrassing excuse to do so.

Indeed, there is a quandary for the institutional church when it claims it has never ordained women. How can it now change that tradition without admitting that they have been wrong all these years? In fact, in 1994 Pope John Paul II made this statement:

Although the teaching that priestly ordination is to be reserved to men alone has been preserved by the constant and universal tradition of the Church, and firmly taught by the *magisterium* in its more recent documents, at the present time in some places it is nonetheless considered still open to debate, or the Church's judgment that women are not to be admitted to ordination is considered to have a merely disciplinary force. Wherefore, in order that all doubt may be removed regarding a matter of great importance, a matter which pertains to the Church's divine constitution itself, in virtue of my ministry of confirming the brethren (cf. Luke 22:32) I declare that the Church has no authority whatsoever to confer priestly ordination on women and that this judgment is to be definitively held by all the Church's faithful (*Ordinatio Sacerdotalis* 4).

Such a forceful dictum that requires the faithful to accept this teaching with "definitive assent" and end any further dialogue or inquiry is severe to a point of incredulity. It also shows a complete lack of understanding of the role of tradition, properly understood, in the life and practice of the Roman Catholic Church. For the institutional church to entertain the notion that such a statement will stop faithful Catholics from questioning and discussing this topic points to a naiveté that is beyond comprehension.

This refusal to ordain women directly affects 50 percent of the church—women—whether they fully accept this attempted silencing or not, because this is a question of power and therefore of justice. It also affects the other 50 percent—us men—whether we fully accept this silencing or not, because it is a question of power and therefore of justice. The treatment by the institutional church of men who are not clerics is closely linked to its treatment of women. I and my fellow brothers can attest to that, as can most other laymen who have anything whatsoever to do with the institutional church.

This kind of "thinking" (rather, perhaps, lack of sound thinking) runs throughout the institutional church and is articulated by some in the hierarchy who are honestly and firmly convinced they are correct in their interpretation that male-only ordination is a matter they cannot change "even if they wanted to." In my opinion, they simply do not properly understand how tradition works in the church. If the institutional church can start baptizing babies, change the rules on usury, "clarify" church teachings on science (talk to Galileo about this), redo the language of the Mass whenever it wants, update the church's position on war and capital punishment, decide what age people should be confirmed, regulate how often people can go to communion and under which species, they can certainly change the rules for who can be ordained.

As always when the institutional church finally makes a change, of course, it will find a rationale for doing so. There is a joke going around liberal circles that says when the institutional church finally does ordain women, it will begin by saying, "As we have always taught…." Who cares? What they will be doing is listening to the voice of the faithful, just as they always eventually do. That is why we have to keep speaking up, even when we have been forbidden to do so.

I, for one, have never doubted the sincerity of those prelates (although neither do I doubt the sincerity of those who do doubt them). What is most frightening about their position is their restrictive understanding of women as "females" instead of "persons," which obfuscates the reality that Jesus, though a male, was also a "person." This lack of clear thinking leads, by extension, to some unfortunate and embarrassing statements from the institutional church. For example, many of the opponents of women's ordination claim that Jesus did not ordain women, therefore the church may not do so either. Of course, Jesus never really "ordained" anyone in the way the church does now, but even assuming that he chose only circumcised men to be priests does not mean that circumcision is a prerequisite for ordination. The church simply relies on tradition to say, "Obviously he did not mean that." Someday they will say the same about women's ordination.

Many faithful Catholics who are neither "liberal" nor "conservative" interpret (fairly or unfairly) the actions of those in charge of the institutional church as being terrified of women, at least women who are their intellectual, spiritual, and (someday) ecclesial equals. That is why I say that women's ordination is about power and therefore justice. Jesus, for example, never established the College of Cardinals and in fact the College of Cardinals used to be made up of laymen (the insistence that they be priests came much later, and even today

Cardinals do not have to be bishops first). If the Vatican wanted to prove that women's ordination is not about power, it could easily change its rule and name women to be 50 percent of the College of Cardinals. You and I know this will not happen, and it will not happen for the same reason that women are not being ordained: It is all about power inside the church.

For many of us, the hierarchical statements that came out of the Vatican regarding the recent so-called "illicit" ordination of Catholic women around the world was difficult to accept. Some Vatican statements categorized these actions as a "grave sin," putting them in the same category as the crime of pedophilia (and its cover-up) in church law. The very sad reality is that many in the curia honestly believe that these two things are equally wrong, but with such statements they prove themselves insensitive to the reactions of many victims of clergy sex abuse. These victims believe that the institutional church for many years employed evasive tactics as it tried to prevent public knowledge of its crimes. To imply that the ordinations of women, even if they were "illicit" by church law, in any way compares to the plight of sex abuse victims is insulting to those victims.

• • • • • •

What is really at stake is that the institutional church does not like strong women.

• • • • • •

Likewise, the sensitivities of women who are truly convinced that the Holy Spirit is calling them to share in Christ's priesthood are also offended by such a comparison. They do not understand how the hierarchy can be so definitively condemnatory of women seeking ordination when they have not been even remotely as disciplinary with clerical pedophiles and their protectors.

What is really at stake is that the institutional church does not like strong women. There is another joke that travels around the "men's club" of the Vatican that says, "We'd ordain women if we could just deny the first thousand women who apply." To which we supporters of women's ordination reply, "You can deny the first thousand women who apply, if we can get rid of the last thousand men you just ordained!"

Such insensitive stances by the institutional church, and the concurrent demand for closure of further dialogue on this topic, unwittingly aligns the church with the pejorative way women are being seen and treated by others around the world. For instance, it becomes more difficult for the institutional church to speak out against the inanity of the statement by a senior Iranian cleric who declared that women who do not dress modestly cause earthquakes, or the statement of Bob Marshall, a Virginia legislator, who said that disabled children are God's punishment for women who had abortions. If the faithful may not even mutter, by official decree of the church, any thought about women's ordination in the church, then why should it surprise us when those responsible for such ridiculous and callous public remarks about women tell the church not to lecture them about women's equality?

A recent study that was sponsored by Trinity College in Dublin surveyed the perception of Irish women about their views of the Catholic Church in comparison to Irish women in Protestant churches. The research concluded that, although these women felt unappreciated by the Catholic Church, nevertheless their faith was still strong. Specifically, 74 percent of the Catholics surveyed believed that the church did not treat them with much respect. Of the Protestant women only 6.3 percent felt that their churches did not treat them respectfully. For the Catholic women 72.3 percent believed that the Catholic Church tries to "control" their position in society, while only 19.7 percent of the Protestant women believed the same of their churches.

A significant focus in helping us understand the quandary for the institutional church regarding the role of women is, of course, the awareness that this attitude is historically embedded within history and culture. Central to the role of women in the church is its long history of public devotion to Mary, the mother of Jesus. More than anything else, official or unofficial, explicit or nuanced, overt or subtle, the understanding of the role of women in the church and the world by the institutional church is conditioned by how it talks, thinks, and theologizes about the Blessed Mother. Therefore, the issue becomes: Is the institutional church, perhaps, too restrictive and confining when it comes to talking and teaching about Mary?

For instance, the institutional church and its hierarchy always speak of Mary as being holy because of her docile, humble, and obedient demeanor to God. Mary's response of commitment when hearing that she was being asked to be the mother of the Messiah—"Be it done unto me according to thy word"—certainly speaks volumes of her faith. These stories of Mary's faithful acquiescence have formed the expectations within the church as to the correct and proper role for women in the church.

But at the same time the institutional church, because of its use of tradition, properly understood, has bestowed on Mary very powerful titles such as "Mediatrix" and "Co-Redemptrix." When the church calls Mary the "Mediatrix of All Graces," it is certainly recognizing this woman's powerful and dynamic role in God's distribution of graces to the world. And, when it speaks of Mary as "Co-Redemptrix," it is stressing the energizing, critical, and creative role of this remarkable woman in Christ's redemption of the human race. Certainly, these attributes of this one woman should qualify other women for the ordained priesthood! The institutional church will remain in its present quandary to the extent it portrays Mary as a passive, submissive, and inactive woman. If, instead, it emphasizes the role and power of Mary in the church, it can use that portrayal as a basis for ordaining women.

• • • • • •

If the institutional church emphasizes the role and power of Mary in the church, it can use that portrayal as a basis for ordaining women.

• • • • • •

In her study on Mary, theologian Sister Elizabeth A. Johnson, CSJ, sets a context of Mary's life regarding the political and economic world of Galilee, the religious world of Second Temple Judaism, and the social and cultural world of women in that place and time. Titled *Truly Our Sister, A Theology of Mary in the Communion of Saints*, Johnson's book helps us imagine Mary in ways that are new and compelling. She develops a Marian theology rooted in scripture and read through women's eyes. This is not a Mary who could be described as some docile and submissive woman; rather, we see a woman who would make a very fine priest today.

Likewise, Margaret George's historical novel *Mary, Called Magdalene* clearly identifies another biblical woman, Mary of Magdala, as another brave, smart woman of considerable substance who was central to Christianity's beginnings. George develops scriptural research that has been "quietly" accepted by the institutional church that negates Magdalene's almost universal image as a reformed prostitute. We must recall that it was Mary Magdalene and other women who witnessed Jesus' death at the foot of the cross (the "chosen" male disciples, all except one, having fled) and Magdalene alone who was the very first to experience the risen Christ. What did she do? She then ran to where the male disciples were hiding to convince them that Jesus had risen from the dead. For this, she was named by Pope John Paul II the "Apostle to the Apostles." But the unfortunate historical distortion of Mary Magdalene's important role in the early church has unquestionably diminished—even to the present day—the vital and dynamic role of all women in the church.

This new biblical and theological scholarship, much of it being done by women themselves, as well as current scientific and psychological evidence on the effects of gender discrimination, has brought to light new and compelling images that will require reasonable leaders within the institutional church to admit the true equality of women in the church, and this must and will require the ordination of women. It seems that the Holy Spirit is "shouting out" to many faithful Catholics and to all people of good will that nothing less than unqualified and full equality is long overdue in the world everywhere. How much more must this be unequivocally manifested in the church and all its structures and ministries?

CHAPTER 10

The Quandary: A Crisis of Conscience

• • • • • •

When a man won't listen to his conscience,
it's usually because he doesn't want advice
from a total stranger.

LINDSEY STEWART

• • • • • •

I hope that the chapters in this book have quite strongly suggested, even to the most casual reader, that the Catholic Church is certainly in the midst of severe and significant upheavals. It is the institutional church leaders who are especially called to get us out of this quandary, with the help of those of us faithful who are willing to articulate our lived experience of the faith.

These church leaders are supposed to be the first and the foremost models of giving witness to how we encounter our neighbors and our enemies with Christian love. Instead, it seems that their incessant, growing preoccupation against relativism gives the appearance that the exercise of their authority is in inverse ratio to their faith in the Holy Spirit's presence in the church. Or perhaps it is in direct ratio to their fear of a possible loss of institutional control. The main point of this book is that they do not really believe in the Catholic concept of tradition, properly understood. They are, in effect, flying in the face of tradition.

In order for the institutional church to unravel the modern day quandary in which it finds itself and lead its people into the world to which the Holy Spirit calls us, it must first understand what is going on in the world and how that necessarily affects the church. A strikingly perceptive insight that can aid us in better grasping this phenomenon is found in a book by author Phyllis Tickle titled *The Great Emergence: How Christianity Is Changing and Why*. There she presents a credible scenario for the dynamics of what is going on in Christianity today as something that happens every five hundred years or so.

Tickle points out that about every five hundred years the church has inevitably been placed in and changed by what she calls giant "rummage sales" caused by the tides of societal change. Certain things are discarded that were once considered treasures, and new things take their place. These strikingly dramatic and significant transformations in the church, of course, have caused much alarm and disruption to the institutional church of the time. But these giant rummage sales have not been stopped, nor have they been diverted by attempted preset outcomes that were programmed by hierarchical decrees. Change has always occurred in the church, usually with much disruption, and it will do so now.

Tickle's study delves into these five hundred year events: The Great Reformation (1517), The Great Schism (1051), The Council of Chalcedon (451). As she points out, Jewish scholars indicate that this half-millennium pattern has also occurred in their particular history. The details of this phenomenon are wonderfully presented in detail in her book, but for purposes here it is sufficient to point out that in Judeo-Christian history significant change has happened quite regularly, about every five hundred years or so, and we are due for another one right about...now! The church that exists today would not be recognized as the same church of two or even one millennia ago, no matter how hard we may try to demonstrate its apparent continuity, and the church of the future will not look like the one of today in 2500 CE.

Tickle contends that we are in the midst of another giant rummage sale... and it ain't gonna be stopped! Oh, it can be ignored. It can be denied. It can be condemned. But it cannot be stopped. The "emerging church" that Tickle describes is coming out of a rummage sale that is affecting all mainline Christian churches, even—and maybe especially—the Catholic Church. Occasioned by the globalization and technological revolution we discussed earlier, this shrinking globe of ours is causing what was previously described as a new "spiritual geography." The emerging Christianity is massive, democratic, dialogical, questioning, instantaneous, engaging, and as Tickle describes it a deeply radical, passionate, non-hierarchical, and non-structured Jesus-oriented movement.

Such an emerging Christianity opens conversations and sharing about Jesus and our personal relationships and encounters with him. Once an emphasis is placed on the interpersonal relationships of people with Jesus, then the primary focus is less on dogmas and more on loving relationships. This is, indeed, a monumental quandary for an institutional church trying to protect what it considers the "deposit of faith" that has been entrusted to it. Of course, when open interpersonal relationships become the norm, then control and doctrine must be transformed into a reliance on the dynamics of *sharing* the person of Jesus rather than placing primary emphasis on structured, doctrinal content that attempts to *explain* Jesus.

• • • • • •

It is not possible to embrace receptivity to the person of Jesus without an open and faith-filled trust in the Spirit's immanent presence in the hearts and minds of the faithful.

• • • • • •

Now enters the Holy Spirit. In this emerging church it is not possible to embrace receptivity to the person of Jesus without an open and faith-filled trust in the Spirit's immanent presence in the hearts and minds of the faithful. This is what I call "tradition, properly understood."

The growing influence and conversions to charismatic and Pentecostal sects around the world, especially in Africa and South America, give credence to the observation that in the new spiritual geography on this globe there is emerging a strong desire for a more personalized encounter with the divine. Criticize as we Catholics might that this is nothing more than emotionalism, nevertheless, millions (not thousands) of people around the world are attracted to this type of spiritual encounter. There is indeed a giant rummage sale taking place in Christianity. The question is this: Can the Catholic Church now transform its processes and structures so that it can be understood by new generations, without losing its core identity? Is the institutional church willing to cast aside its old operational structures and acknowledge that elements that are humanly constructed—not divinely instituted—will need a giant rummage sale of the perks and practices of its current institutional organization? Are our church leaders, in essence, willing to demonstrate in fact and not just in word that they are the servants of the People of God and not their masters?

Even in 2004 Pope John Paul II recognized it was not just some of the usual malcontents who were creating the problems he and most in the hierarchy had come to expect in the church. The problems that arose from such people were always present and certainly annoying, but they were always absorbed within the everyday workings of the institutional church without serious disruption. In fact, for many in the hierarchy these kinds of clashes were viewed as good opportunities to trumpet their views and, since the media relished controversy, this gave them a good platform from which to sound off with their own spin on these topics.

However, the latest threats have certainly not been "business as usual" for the institutional church because of:

- The mounting sex abuse scandals becoming public; and
- The cover-ups by bishops and their underlings trying to protect the church's reputation rather than first protecting the child victims; and
- An overwhelming majority of the faithful disagreeing or ignoring the institutional church's teachings on birth control, homosexuality, and other sexual matters; and
- A sizeable movement pushing for priests and laypeople electing their own bishops as had been done in the early church; and
- A growing call for married priests; and
- Strong sentiment for the acceptance of priestly ordination for women.

In fact, on September 11, 2004, speaking to the bishops from dioceses in Pennsylvania and New Jersey on their *ad limina* meeting in the Vatican, John Paul II spoke in terms of "...the crisis of confidence in the church's leadership provoked by the recent sexual abuse scandals, [and] the general call for accountability in the church's governance on every level and in the relations between bishops, clergy, and the lay faithful."

Thus, the institutional church knew the "problem" was no longer being caused by some malcontents speaking out against the church. This was a "crisis in confidence" among the faithful. The pope knew the "problem" then. The bishops knew the "problem" then. The curia knew the "problem" then.

• • • • • •

Why did not the institutional church respond effectively in order to correct the problem in an appropriately timely fashion?

• • • • • •

So, the quandary is: Why did not the institutional church respond effectively in order to correct the problem in an appropriately timely fashion?

This pervasive crisis in confidence has continued to grow, and the response from many in the hierarchy is still to blame the media, secularists, and the "dictatorship of relativism" for the continued worldwide attacks on the church. The knee-jerk reaction of institutional church leaders has been to seek refuge in the idea that "quality is more important than quantity" and that "the church needs to get smaller but more orthodox." I would say that most of the men I know in the hierarchy are truly convinced that that is a correct analysis. They believe they are defending the values and religious beliefs of the faith and must simply "stay the course." That is why I have found it necessary to write this book.

A story told by Anthony de Mello, SJ, in his book *The Song of the Bird* might shed some light on this quandary in which the church finds itself. He tells the story about the devil and his friend going for a walk:

They saw a man ahead of them stoop down and pick up something from the road. "What did that man find?" asked the friend.

"A piece of truth," said the devil.

"Doesn't that disturb you?" asked the friend.

"No it does not," said the devil. "I shall allow him to make a religious belief out of it."

For de Mello, it was important that we be aware of this reality. He explained: "A religious belief is a signpost pointing the way to truth. People who cling tenaciously to the signpost are prevented from moving towards the truth because they have the false feeling that they already possess it."

So much of the difficulty and distress we see today in the church can be healed if none of us act as if we have a monopoly on truth. The dogmas, doctrines, and pronouncements of religion are mere signposts pointing to the truth. The truth is the grace of the Holy Spirit alive in the minds and hearts of the faithful, and this is reflected in the lived experience of the faithful, which I have called here "tradition, properly understood."

What is so astounding and incomprehensible to me is that if you listen to the proclamations coming from the institutional church leaders they say many of these very things I am saying, but their practice does not reflect their words. For instance, the 2003 Post-Synodal Apostolic Exhortation *Pastores Gregis* insists that all a bishop says and does must reveal Christ's way of acting (see PG 43). It then continues and exhorts each bishop to develop a pastoral style which is ever more open to collaboration with all and presupposes the participation of every category of the faithful in as much as they share responsibility for the good of the particular local church which they themselves form (see PG 44). It further describes the bishop as a "promoter of justice and peace, model and promoter of the spirituality of communion, model of attentive listening, and a person of dialogue." (PG 19)

These are wonderful exhortations that if heeded and exercised by those in the institutional church most likely would resolve the current turmoil. It is time for the church to begin being *communio*. To accomplish this we all—faithful and hierarchy alike—must match our words with our actions.

John F. Kavanaugh, SJ, a professor of philosophy at St. Louis University, in an article in *America* (September 13, 2010) related similar thoughts. Speaking of Pope Benedict XVI's encyclical *Deus Caritas Est*, Kavanaugh noted that Benedict considers love to be the "indispensable expression" of the church's very being. Kavanaugh says that, "The encyclical's inspiring words are often not matched by the reality." He says that "…we should be honest with ourselves, especially, when considering the church as institution and how it is perceived in the world." Even more troubling for all is Kavanaugh's stark statement:

Indeed, there have been members of the hierarchy who, like Archbishop Mark Coleridge in Australia, have worried about a "clericalism understood as a hierarchy of power, not service." But there is at least a perception among many Catholics (including the 10 percent who have left the church in the last decade) that power is a greater concern to members of the hierarchy than service to "proclaiming the words of the sacraments" and "the ministry of charity."

A beautiful expression of a bishop's way to administer to the People of God was offered in *Pastores Gregis*, when it says:

Hope in Jesus the Good Shepherd will fill [a bishop's] heart with compassion, prompting him to draw near to the pain of every suffering man and woman and to soothe their wounds, ever confident that every lost sheep will be found." (PG 4)

That is the kind of leadership I am looking for from the institutional church, and that is where I will end this book. In my next one, I will explore how Catholic education might be another tool for unraveling the quandary that the church has gotten itself into. For now, I just want to say that I believe that the Holy Spirit will lead us out of it, using the power of tradition, properly understood.

EPILOGUE

A Voice of Tradition

. . . . . .

Don't be discouraged by anxieties and troubles.
Life is full of them.

SAINT JOHN BAPTIST DE LASALLE

. . . . . .

On May 24, 1950, a 17th century Frenchman who never stepped foot outside of France, a priest and person admired for his kindness, faithfulness, and intellectual refinement, was proclaimed by the church "Patron of All Teachers of Youth." His name was John Baptist De LaSalle, who was born into a family of considerable means. Coming from such a privileged family, he was expected to excel in whatever area of pursuit he decided upon for his future.

Young John decided early in his life that he had a vocation to the priesthood. Given his family's wealth and prominence, it was not unusual that he was given the benefit of the finest formation, education, and clerical advancement opportunities. So advantaged was this cultivated young man that even before he was ordained a priest he was named Canon of the Cathedral Church of Reims—a good indication that he was on track to an eventual bishop's miter, since this assignment was the breeding ground for bishops and cardinals in the French church during that time.

In 1669 student John Baptist De LaSalle earned his master's degree with highest honors. The following year he entered the seminary of Saint Sulpice in Paris. In 1678 he received a licentiate degree in theology, and the same year he was ordained a priest. He continued his studies and in 1680 received his doctorate degree in theology.

Now this 27-year-old young man's career was set and made. The remainder of his life could then be one of comfort, prestige, and freedom to pursue his interests with ease. He had wealth, education, position, and the privileged clerical state in hand. He was, by definition, a member of the institutional church.

However, the life of John Baptist De LaSalle became anything but the life of a 17th century privileged French cleric, for he threw his lot in with the faithful of his time.

Only one year after his ordination, he became acquainted with the work of the Sisters of the Child Jesus. These Sisters were dedicated to providing schooling for poor children. While helping them, De LaSalle encountered a layman, Adrian Nyel, who had been asked by a wealthy widow to start a school for poor boys. John proved to be helpful to Nyel by introducing him to people of means and power who helped open this school.

Soon after that, another wealthy woman approached Nyel and offered to fund a school for the poor, but only if LaSalle would be involved in this endeavor. John agreed, and so began his lifetime interest in and engagement with schools for the poor, rather than as a probable prestigious prelate of the church.

And so too did John Baptist De LaSalle's transformative work in education bring him into sharp conflict with the upper social classes, with civic rulers, and especially with church authorities. How could it be that so many of them would be upset with someone who was only responding to God's call to help the poor? Or as he would say it, "I adore in all things God's will in my life." God was calling him to serve the poor, as was the calling of the church in its totality; yet John was confronted with significant resistance all his life.

By reviewing De LaSalle's actions as he became active in schooling for the poor, I have come to understand the animosity that grew around his transformative initiatives. Education at that time was only affordable to the wealthy. The poor could not gain access to appropriate schooling in which they could acquire the knowledge and skills to become productive members of society's power base. Nor were those in society's privileged classes, including the institutional church at that time, interested in diminishing their power by having educated poor people diluting their influential status. Those with knowledge and skills were those with the power in those days, as they are today, and therefore they were the ones who controlled the wealth, the economy, the society… and the church. In essence, the same principle that is still a familiar refrain to this day was prominent and foremost in society's advantaged classes then: The rich get rich and the poor get poorer!

Access to education in those days was mainly for the wealthy, as is becoming true again today. At that time the "technology" of teaching was the tutorial method, and few could afford that. The expense incurred by a family to hire individual tutors as teachers for their children was impossible for any except the most wealthy. (Think what is happening in many school systems today!) Thus a vicious loop was embedded in society, which insured that education would never be open to the poor.

• • • • • •

John Baptist De LaSalle became an imaginative and innovative societal agent for transformation society by challenging and changing the church.

• • • • • •

However, John Baptist De LaSalle, a well-to-do "gentleman cleric," became an imaginative and innovative societal agent for transformation of a system that imprisoned the poor with a life sentence of oppression or at least marginalization within society. And he did so by challenging and changing the church.

So it was that in 1680 he began to take action to remedy this situation. De LaSalle took into his well-established and comfortable home a group of men who were not educated tutors but struggling teachers who wanted to help the disadvantaged. It is important to stress that these men were not the refined, educated, and professional type that were teaching the wealthy. Rather they were faithful and faith-filled Catholic laymen, who lacked social graces or training and as such were looked-down upon by the privileged classes. These men John took into his own home and fed them and trained them to be teachers.

At this point, his family, friends, and fellow clerics were scandalized at this unheard of, uncouth, and unorthodox way of being church. After all, for the well-to-do at that time it was unheard of that a priest with such a privileged background would lower himself and make commoners his equal colleagues. This did not stop him. 1680 is considered to be the founding of The Institute of the Brothers of the Christian Schools (*Fratres Scholarum Cristianarum*) or, as we are now commonly referred to, the "De LaSalle Brothers," a group I joined over forty years ago and have served with side-by-side since then.

John Baptist De LaSalle was able to attract and train these barely literate laymen into a cohesive yet struggling community who dedicated themselves to found and conduct schools for the poor without charging for their services. In 1683 he decided that he was called by God to be more like his "brothers" in their poverty and dependence on God's providence, so he made an unexpected decision. He renounced all his wealth. But instead of giving it to his community for their schools, as you might expect, he gave away all he had in order to feed the poor during a severe famine that was then victimizing France. This action did not sit well with all his colleagues. Many thought his wealth should go to their own schools and for their own support. Tensions among his own brothers against his actions and decisions grew, but John would continue to follow the will of God as he saw it.

Tensions grew from outside constituencies as well. He opened many new schools throughout France and attracted more laymen to the community. His free schools were open to all, and their popularity also increased among the non-poor. As the popularity of his free schools grew, he encountered many new and serious problems. Instead of others encouraging and assisting him and his new approach to education for the poor, attacks and disdain for De LaSalle increased.

At that time, there were businesses in which teachers were available to those who could afford to pay their fees. These fee-taking teachers grew hostile to De LaSalle's free schools, since they were taking work from them. They filed suits in the courts against these schools and claimed they were operating in violation of the laws and regulations. For years these legal battles continued, and some of the lawsuits were decided against him. Though at times he became distressed, nevertheless John steadfastly continued in his transformative work.

Perhaps the most distressful and offensive resistance to De LaSalle's educational work with the poor came from the unlikeliest of places: the institutional church's hierarchical authorities. De LaSalle did not have any explicit church approval to operate these free schools, so they were not under the direct control of the ecclesiastical church authorities of the time. Considerable friction arose because in many instances charitable financial support, which was formerly given to parishes and diocesan treasuries, was directed to De LaSalle's schools instead. Nothing makes the institutional church more upset than that, even to this day!

John experienced tension, hostility, harassment, and legal entanglements from within his own community, civic authorities, business concerns, and the institutional church—all at the same time. This would be enough to stop most people from continuing a pursuit, no matter how noble it may have been, but it did not stop this John Baptist De LaSalle. He continued to do the will of God as he saw it, with a faith in God's call and with zeal to take action in order to make real where the Spirit was leading him. He was an "exercise in tradition, properly understood."

• • • • • •

De LaSalle continued to do the will of God as he saw it, with a faith in God's call and with zeal to take action in order to make real where the Spirit was leading him.

• • • • • •

Today no one in the church doubts that Saint John Baptist De LaSalle was indeed a pioneer, innovator, and transformative leader, not only as a religious educator but also in the total spectrum of education in general. Even recognizing these accomplishments would not accurately portray the fullness of what this man accomplished, however. Though he has not been commonly recognized as such, De LaSalle was really an institutional church transformational agent. His effectiveness in initiating and sustaining educational change led to practical and pragmatic ways the church did education. It changed the poor and working class faithful from indentured servants of the privileged to people with skills and knowledge, bestowing upon them a dignity that would become embedded in a newly liberated and educated Catholic laity.

The prayerful and persistent De LaSalle transformed what it meant to be a member of the Catholic Church. No longer were faithful lay members of the church merely docile and dependent upon a "learned" clergy. They became people of God with faith and zeal of their own and an education to go along with it. Almost single-handedly, John Baptist De LaSalle changed the "lived experience of the faithful."

De LaSalle transformed Christian education with its focus on "other worldly" types of spirituality to one that developed the full potential of each individual. His schools broke down social class and financial barriers. While never detracting from the spiritual and salvific inspiration of his educational mission, he successfully incorporated and cultivated an academic curriculum that was both practical and effective by engaging his students in preparation for the society that had previously afforded them very little hope of sustaining themselves with even a modicum of dignity.

His revolutionary methods provided that teaching in his schools would be done exclusively in the vernacular instead of the classical languages of Latin and Greek as was prevalent at that time. This facilitated what can be described as the democratization of education, making it possible for commoners to have access to excellent education. Also, in De LaSalle schools he developed effectively the "simultaneous methodology" of teaching groups of students together instead of the more costly "tutorial" pedagogy.

He continued his innovative methods by breaking down social barriers and class status in his schools. As his schools became more popular and the advantaged classes started to send their children to them because they were superior, De LaSalle had students of all social classes studying, playing, praying, and eating together. He continued his outreach and commitment to democratizing schools by beginning a training school for all teachers who were interested in learning his innovative educational strategies and methods.

Saint John Baptist De LaSalle steadfastly and with faith and zeal committed himself to the transformation of both the church and civil society through education, even though he continued to be harassed and challenged on each step of his journey. John accomplished what can appropriately be described as a revolutionary transformation in the church and society, because he dared to re-imagine how things should be and had the faith to listen to what God was calling him to do and act upon it.

In fact De LaSalle, reflecting on all the resistance he received while trying to do good, wrote: "For my own part, I tell you now that if God had revealed to me all the labor and the crosses that were to accompany any good I was to do in founding the Brothers of the Christian Schools, my courage would have failed. I have been persecuted by the Church, by those from whom I had every right to expect help. My own Brothers, those whom I cherish with the utmost tenderness, whom I trained with greatest care and affection, and to whom I looked for help in serving the poor, rose up against me."

When you know the story of St. John Baptist De LaSalle, it is not difficult to understand that when someone tries to transform the institutional church he or she will probably get into some kind of trouble. This is why I have had whatever courage it might have taken to write this book. For I am one of John's "Brothers," and after 300 years we are still committed to speaking the truth and doing what needs to be done to continue spreading the Good News of Jesus Christ to all people.

I would like to finish with a prayer I wrote and pray almost every day. I think it sums up what I have been trying to communicate in this book. It begins on the next page.

• • • • • •

A Prayer for Tradition

Lord, I do not understand why you permit suffering in this life.

I do not understand why you permit evil in this world.

I do not understand why you allow division in your church.

But...

*I do understand that my faith in you
and your unconditional love for all creation
gives meaningfulness to that suffering, evil, and division
in spite of my limitations in understanding.*

**So I pray—this I do believe.
And may Jesus live in our hearts forever.**

*Lord, I do not understand why sometimes I doubt
your presence in me.*

*I do not understand why sometimes I doubt
your presence in the world.*

*I do not understand why sometimes I even doubt
your presence in your church.*

But...

*I do understand that my doubts are not a sign of my lack of faith;
rather they are the sacrament of your presence in me
that make it possible to live a faith-filled life in spite of those doubts.*

**So I pray—this I do believe.
And may Jesus live in our hearts forever.**

*Lord, I do not understand how it is humanly possible
for any person in this world to be infallible.*

*I do not understand how any institution in this world
can always be right.*

I do not understand how on this shrinking globe of ours,
with new knowledge and insights being discovered each day,
how any doctrine can remain unquestioned and unexplored
since your Spirit is teaching the minds
and touching the hearts
of the faithful each day.

But...

I do understand that my faith in your church
gives meaningfulness to the infallibility of the magisterium
that is inspired by your Holy Spirit.

I do understand an infallibility made real only through a magisterium
that embraces a solemn, trusting, sensitive and open listening
to all the People of God.

So I pray—this I do believe.
And may Jesus live in our hearts forever.

Lord, I do not understand why the institutional church
too often issues commands to the People of God
instead of speaking with compassion and acceptance for all,
even the sinners, the unorthodox, and those who disagree with it.

I do not understand why the institutional church
too often only hears those who agree with it
instead of listening to the anguish and longing of those it has excluded.

I do not understand why the institutional church
too often sees the kaleidoscopic array of diversity
of cultures and religions in this world
but does not perceive that it is in the embracing of that diversity
that unity is achieved.

But ...

I do understand that as the sinful prodigal son
was joyfully welcomed home to his father's house,
so too should the church find ways to welcome home
the divorced, gay men and women, women seeking priestly ordination,
and all the children of God it has deemed "unfit" to be Catholic.

I do understand that the Holy Spirit will guide the church
and will raise up the prophets and leaders
so that the People of God will speak, listen, perceive, and invite
all people to become sisters and brothers of one another.

So I pray—this I do believe.
And may Jesus live in our hearts forever.

Lord, I do not understand why there has to be
a conservative way to belong to your church.

I do not understand why there has to be
a liberal way to experience your church.

I do not understand why there has to be

only one way to be church.

But...

I do understand that in the beauty, peace, and harmony
of your Creation variety abounds.
I do understand that through, with, and in your very own Triune differences
you achieve unity.

I do understand that it is only through, with, and in the many differences
inside the church that we all may be one with you.

So I pray—this I do believe.
And may Jesus live in our hearts forever.

Amen, Alleluia

ACKNOWLEDGMENTS

This book would not have been possible if it were not for the personal support and inspiration throughout the years from many colleagues and institutions that I have been blessed to know and with whom I have worked. Foundationally, I am grateful for the continuous spiritual and intellectual sustenance that I have experienced as a De LaSalle Christian Brother for more than four decades of my life. My De LaSalle confreres throughout the world have modeled for me what it means to be Catholic and Christian. Their lives of faith and zeal model a rich and magnificent diversity as loyal members of the Roman Catholic Church, which sometimes includes being constructively critical. For twenty-one of those years, from 1984-2005, I enjoyed academic and intellectual nourishment from the faculty, staff, and trustees as President of Saint Mary's University of Minnesota.

There are several individuals to whom I am indebted for their excellent and direct assistance to me on this project. During the writing of the first drafts of this work, Professor Emeritus Michael G. Flanagan, PhD., of Saint Mary's University of Minnesota, did an outstanding job of editing the entire manuscript. I appreciated his patience and attention to detail during his work on the text.

It was a pleasure to work with a gifted theologian who reviewed the entire work and provided me with excellent observations and suggestions on many theological questions that arose. Cynthia A. Nienhaus, CSA, PhD., Assistant Professor of Theology at Marian University, was exceptional in her review and critique. Sister Cynthia devoted a great deal of time carefully examining the manuscript and offering me keen and insightful recommendations. However, in no manner does this necessarily imply that she agrees with my observations or conclusions.

I was fortunate to receive wonderful advice concerning the continuity and clarity of the text from Mary Catherine Fox, PhD., Professor of Interdisciplinary Studies at Saint Mary's University of Minnesota. She carefully examined the entire text so that I was able to make some very complex material more clearly understandable.

Also, in order to present my observations with a broader perspective than I would be able to accomplish alone, I had the excellent insight and views from three persons that I respect for their religious and global sensitivities. Gary F. Gleason, MS, Canon to the Ordinary of the Episcopal Diocese of Minnesota, retired, and currently Principal Consultant of the Gleason Group, Minneapolis, was a resourceful and insightful contributor. Irma M. Wyman, EngD., Corporate Vice President of Honeywell, Inc., retired, and Archdeacon of the Episcopal Diocese of Minnesota, retired, was a helpful and fine reader of the manuscript. And I am grateful to my colleague in Rome, Dott. Alessandro Lombardi, who was a thoughtful, rigorous, and precise reviewer of the entire manuscript.

I am most indebted to Gregory Pierce, publisher of ACTA Publications, who provided excellent final editing of the manuscript and many thoughtful and keen insights that made this work a more clear and cogent presentation.

Each of these persons was an invaluable personal resource and professional assistance that helped make this project a reality. I am truly in their debt, and I am grateful for their critiques, which were pleasant yet always direct and candid.

However, any shortcomings or deficiencies in this book are directly and totally mine. All the views and positions that I present in this work are also totally mine. No person or institution that I have had the honor to be associated with is necessarily in agreement with views that are expressed in this work.

BOOKS OF RELATED INTEREST

GREAT AMERICAN CATHOLIC EULOGIES
Compiled and introduced by Carol DeChant
Foreword by Thomas Lynch

Fifty eulogies, printed memorials, and elegiac poems that give a real feel for the "lived experience" of American Catholics from colonial times to the present.

INVITATION TO CATHOLICISM
INVITATION TO THE OLD TESTAMENT
INVITATION TO THE NEW TESTAMENT
Alice Camille

Three companion books by award-winning author Alice Camille that offer clear, concise, and informative explanations of the Catholic understanding of Tradition and Scripture.

CHURCH, CHICAGO-STYLE
William L. Droel
Foreword by Sr. Patricia Crowley, OSB

A celebration of the history of active clerical leadership and lay involvement in the Catholic Church in Chicago over the last fifty years. 126-page paperback, $12.95

SPIRITUALITY AT WORK
THE MASS IS NEVER ENDED
THE WORLD AS IT SHOULD BE
Gregory F. Augustine Pierce

Three books that examine the whats, whys, and hows of the mission of all Christians to help bring about the kingdom of God "on earth, as it is in heaven."

RUNNING INTO THE ARMS OF GOD
THE GEOGRAPHY OF GOD'S MERCY
THE LONG YEARNING'S END
Patrick Hannon, CSC

This trilogy of award-winning stories of the presence of God in daily life by one of the best storytellers in the American Catholic Church.

Available from Booksellers or 800-397-2282
www.actapublications.com